LEADING
MEDICAL GROUP
TRANSFORMATION

VIC ARNOLD • MATTHEW BATES

Published by:
Fire Starter Publishing
350 West Cedar Street
Suite 300
Pensacola, FL 32502
Phone: 866-354-3473
Fax: 850-332-5117
www.firestarterpublishing.com

ISBN: 978-1-62218-084-4

Library of Congress Control Number: 2017933777

TABLE OF CONTENTS

INTRODUCTION

A Word from the Authors

If you've picked up this book, you are most likely either a leader of a physician organization or a health system leader who works closely with one. Either way, you are tasked with guiding physician organizations into a future that's experiencing faster, more extreme change than we've seen unfold over the past century.

Reimbursement rules and shifting consumer expectations are forcing us all to rethink the way we deliver care in a medical practice. Team-based care is becoming prevalent, with nurse practitioners and physician assistants becoming primary clinicians.

Urgent care access points are springing up on every street corner. Telehealth setups, where physicians and patients connect via digital data exchange platforms and video chat, are becoming more widely used and accepted. Older physicians are retiring, and new ones with different expectations and values are taking their place.

And so on. These are just a few of the forces that are shaking up our industry. And who knows what future changes lie in store?

One thing's for sure: Whether you've been in your leadership role for 20 years or were just hired this morning, it is unlikely anyone would have mastered all the skills needed to meet the new demands being generated on an almost daily basis. This book is designed to help you close those gaps.

Based on Huron's and Studer Group's decades of experience working with healthcare systems and medical groups of all sizes—including non-traditional medical groups such as hospitalist organizations, AMCs, CINs, FQHCs, and RHCs—*Leading Medical Group Transformation* will provide a solid overview of what it takes to run a practice and run it well. Obviously, we can't provide all the answers in this short book, but we can help you start to ask the right questions.

We can promise you that you'll learn new ways to think about a variety of vital issues: from selecting and training great leaders to building a patient-centric practice to creating a carefully strategized brand to engaging your physicians, employees, and patients.

You may find it valuable to read this book cover to cover. Or you might choose to turn immediately to the chapters that connect to your most pressing pain points. Either way, thank you for reading our book. We hope it helps you navigate a future whose only constant is change.

Vic Arnold
Matthew Bates

CHAPTER 1

Today's Transforming Medical Group:
The "Front Door" to a Rapidly Shifting Landscape

> "It is not the strongest of the species that survives, nor the most intelligent that survives. It is the one that is most adaptable to change."
> —Charles Darwin

The way our nation thinks about healthcare has undergone a fundamental shift. It only stands to reason that the organizations that comprise the industry's collective "front door"—the medical groups—must *also* transform the way they operate.

We all know change is rarely embraced. Indeed, there's something in human nature that actively resists it. That's why, for medical group leaders and healthcare system executives who can't (or won't) bend to accommodate shifting market forces, the age we're living in feels worse than challenging. It can feel like a potential extinction event. Yet for those who are embracing change, it feels like a time of tremendous transformation and opportunity.

We wrote this book for the optimists, the action-takers, the forge-aheaders—or at least those who want to fit these descriptors. Studer Group®, a Huron solution, has worked with hundreds of medical groups and healthcare systems over the past decade. Our goal is to help our clients better design, manage, and collaborate with leaders both within their own medical practices as well as with the health systems, hospitals, and other physician organizations in their communities to optimize patient engagement and build or maintain market share. In the process, we have learned exactly how the successful players are responding to the massive changes that are shaking up our industry.

Now, this book is going to lay out some very specific how-tos that apply to the medical group itself *and* to the health system that it's affiliated with—leading practices from high performing organizations. But before we get there, we are going to address the *whys*. By that we mean *why* we wrote this book and *why* healthcare leaders like you will benefit from reading it. The *whys* boil down to three ominous words, inspired by Charles Darwin: *Change or die!*

The Time to Change Is *NOW*

We all know that the healthcare marketplace is moving rapidly toward value-based reimbursement models for patient care. In addition, patients are becoming ever more responsible for the actual cost of the care they receive due to changes in their personal and employer-sponsored healthcare. This means there are several fundamental changes that you need to make in every aspect of your health system and/or medical group. This is not just a patient billing change but rather a move back toward putting patients first at all times. It sounds straightforward, doesn't it? Yet for most organizations it is *not*.

If you're like most of us, you've been in a position where you know you need to make some big, sweeping change in some area of your life. You *know* it in your bones—yet you try really hard not to *know* that you know it. Call it denial or procrastination or simply the choice to distract yourself with other issues rather than taking the hard steps that will rock your world in the short term (even though, in the long term, these steps will take you away from the threat and place you and your practice in a position to thrive in the changing market).

This is exactly where many health systems and medical groups are right now. Yet from where we stand, here on the ragged edge of the healthcare quake, we can clearly see the precariousness of your position. If you don't make the right big change—and if the timing isn't exactly right, and if you don't prepare the organization for that change in advance—you'll likely be out of business (or part of another business) in the next several years.

It *is* that serious. But it's not impossible. We don't want you to be reluctant to embark on the needed journey because we are here to walk you through exactly what you need to do next—and after that—and after that.

First, let's touch on a few realities that are forcing all of us to change the way we operate.

Physician Employment Is *PAST* Its Tipping Point

Number one: Physician employment isn't merely at a tipping point; it has already tipped over. More than two-thirds of all physicians self-identified as employed in 2016.[1] In addition, "splitters" are diminishing as physicians are increasingly financially tied to one health system.

Like every other industry, healthcare is undergoing massive consolidation. Health systems are acquiring and affiliating with physician practices, and physician practices are letting it happen at an unprecedented pace. Actually, we hesitate to use the word "acquired" as it implies an owner/owned relationship and that's really not what we are talking about. What is being created is actually a potentially powerful partnership in which everyone benefits—including (not incidentally) our patients.

Physicians want this partnership because they need shelter from a raging economic and regulatory storm. In many cases, their income has dropped dramatically. They can no longer cope alone with astronomical regulatory changes (think MACRA, ACA, etc.), administrative burdens like electronic health records (EHRs) that don't follow how they practice, and overhead requirements that must be met whether they're one of three physicians or 3,000 physicians.

Health systems want the partnership too. They must attract and retain patients in order to meet their revenue, capital, and market needs. Therefore they are actively executing on strategies aimed at acquiring and optimizing their physician networks of specialists and primary care physicians. In some markets this is manifesting as progress toward clinically integrated networks of employed and affiliated physicians. In others, the health systems are fighting non-traditional competitors like insurance companies and others to affiliate with and support medical groups.

Why Physician Employment? Let Us Count the Reasons

Obviously, the trend toward physician employment is happening for a reason—actually many reasons. Despite the drawbacks to the new arrangement (and yes, there are some very real ones), both physicians themselves and healthcare systems are benefiting. Let's take a quick look at the advantages for both parties.

Why Physicians Want to Be Employees:

1. It provides financial security.
   a. Salaries reduce income risk and uncertainty. Physicians know how much money they're going to make and can plan and live accordingly.
   b. Shifting malpractice insurance and other material costs to an organization reduces an individual physician's financial burden and the need to absorb unplanned increases.
   c. Being employed shifts much of the financial risk of value-based payment and accountable care payment models from the physician to the medical group.
2. It can allow for a better work-life blend.
   a. Employment models support flexible scheduling options. This includes the ability to increase/decrease work hours over time and potentially take extended vacations.
   b. The ability to share being "on call" among the employed group greatly reduces the number of night/weekend disruptions.
   c. While both genders value their "family time," it's probably no coincidence that work-life blend is increasing in focus at a time when medical schools now enroll more women than men.
3. It reduces administrative work.
   a. Physicians can hand off the administrative tasks and get back to the business of being doctors.

b. The burden of negotiating and working with payers is shifted to administrators. Also, employment greatly reduces the risk of being cut from a key payer's preferred network.

c. It offloads some of the administrative hassle of managing an electronic health record and achieving "meaningful use."

d. Value-based payment pressure on payments from CMS and private payers means that participation in some programs (MACRA for example) is becoming ever more complicated and difficult to manage as an independent physician.

Why Health Systems Want to Employ Physicians:

1. It helps them capture more patient referrals.

   a. Obviously, the more doctors on their payroll, the more referrals they can capture.

   b. Employed clinicians keep a higher percent of referrals in "their" health system versus splitting them between systems.

   c. They have an edge in the "arms race." Hiring physicians quickly keeps the competition from scooping them up and capturing their referrals.

2. It facilitates value-based payment program participation.

   a. Many forms of value-based payment are rewarding care across the care continuum (e.g., bundles), requiring tighter coordination and controls between different delivery types.

   b. As payers provide population-based payment adjustments (e.g., MACRA), the need to capture and coordinate data across the care continuum is increasing as are the challenges of coordinating care across different EHRs.

3. It increases their negotiating power with payers.

   a. The bigger a system is, the more negotiating power they have—whether they're at the table with insurance companies or setting prices for their services with large employers.

   b. Larger health systems also have more leverage to ensure they are included in payers' and employers' preferred networks.

In addition, the need for acute care is shrinking due to advances in clinical medicine (consider oncology and orthopedics to list two), so many health systems are adapting to reflect a more outpatient-centric and ambulatory organization model. The upshot is that connecting the entire continuum of care across all settings is more than just a flavor-of-the-month topic these days.

Of course, this trend toward physician employment is being driven by market forces. The fact that payer models are relentlessly and rapidly moving from pay-for-volume to value-based/alternative payment models—which depend on clinical and patient experience outcomes—looms large. MACRA and the other value-based payment programs are concrete examples of how the market can change quickly—and how, overall, the basis of reimbursement is moving rapidly toward value-based alternative payment models.

We've come a long way since the days when the country doctor helped deliver the baby in exchange for a chicken. It's a bit of an oversimplification, but now rather than getting paid for what they do, healthcare providers are getting paid for *how well* they do things—and only for those things that can actually demonstrate value based on concrete evidence.

Obviously, this shift in how we're reimbursed changes everything about how healthcare systems and physician practices operate, both independently and together. The upside here is the ability to focus more tightly and accurately on value and outcomes rather than just "making the turnstiles turn faster" and burning out providers. And as the presence of value-based reimbursement models grows in both the government and commercial payer sectors (and it surely will), the need to make such changes will become more and more urgent.

A Technology-Fueled Consumer Coup Is in Full Force

What's more, consumers in general are really feeling their power, and patients are no exception. This is one of the main drivers of the need for change. Patients have changed their view of what is acceptable in terms of access, quality, and service from physicians. In the past, for example, a two-day wait to see a physician was not considered unreasonable. Now, same day (or even same *hour*) access is the expectation.

As value-based reimbursement models increasingly link the patient experience to reimbursement, hospitals and physician practices alike will need to make changes aimed at improving their quality of care scoring via vehicles like HEDIS, MACRA, HCAHPS, and CG CAHPS results, respectively. This really means building the practice around the patient rather than the provider. And since these survey results are or will be publicly reported, it's easy to go online and compare the patient friendliness of healthcare organizations.

This scoring will also have increasing sway over individual physician affiliation and acquisition decisions by health systems, so there is a direct need to rapidly accelerate the learning curve for improving results. Finally, changing how patients perceive the delivery of care is tough. Making sure there is appropriate and timely communication between provider and patient is more critical than ever.

Technology is driving other changes in consumer behavior as well. The rise of the smartphone has enabled positive, dramatic changes in access and availability of care. Patients can access their or other qualified providers via their smartphone, tablet, or laptop to have quick, low-acuity consultations that can improve overall health status and create greater patient engagement. The digitization of healthcare services improves the ability of the patient/consumer to directly access care in ways that were not really thought possible less than five years ago.

An article in *Healthcare Finance News* covered a presentation by Cardiologist Eric Topol at HFMA's 2016 Annual National Institute. Dr. Topol described and/or demonstrated the use of smartphones to self-administer ultrasounds and a (not yet FDA approved) watch to take blood pressure—among other self-diagnosing, self-monitoring, money-saving technological advances.

He was quoted as saying, "...Democratization of medicine, giving people more charge of their health, of their medical data, of only their medical data. That's going to happen now that they can generate a lot of it. It's inevitable. This is a flip, an inversion of medicine as it's been practiced for over two millennia."[2]

Clearly, technology can be a powerful enabler for more efficient, effective patient care. Yet, the bad news is that technology is also a barrier to efficiency. While EHRs, for example, are intended to increase efficiency, too often their current design impedes patient and physician engagement while overburdening the practice with administrative tasks that did not previously exist. This is the current paradox of technology in healthcare.

Along with the issues created by the EHR, there is the paradox that is the Internet. It too can be a barrier to efficient care. Due to the ubiquity and low quality of organized medical information online, patients are likely to research their own conditions and treatments and play an ever more active role in shaping their own care, often to their own detriment. Meanwhile, current regulations heavily restrict direct electronic communication between patients and their care providers—thanks to privacy protections that are, frankly, outdated.

The problem of inaccurate information falling into the hands of patients aside, the Internet also provides a path to improve patient engagement and physician satisfaction. The pace of the digitization of healthcare continues. One of the best examples will be seen as telehealth services reemerge in a more mature and simplified delivery model; state laws and regulations are starting to catch up. While this can be seen as a disruptive force, it also can be a way to provide care in a more convenient and efficient setting.

Healthcare Coverage Changes Are Also Shaping Consumer Behavior

Finally, changes in healthcare coverage can present a barrier to the delivery of timely and well-designed patient care. For a variety of reasons, patients are paying more and more of the cost of their care out of pocket. High-deductible coverage, while a good way to control costs in some instances, also creates an incentive not to seek timely care in the right setting.

Witness the rise of the free-standing ED services that depend on the new plans to extract large payments from patients when they could or should have been seen in a lower intensity urgent care, retail clinic, telehealth, or traditional office-based practice. Because of high deductibles and the barrier to care they can present, patients are too often going to the ED (freestanding or otherwise) for acute conditions that could have been prevented with timely intervention.

None of this is surprising: Unintended consequences are always a side effect of progress. Sorting out how to structure the changing "footprint" of care delivery that is designed with the patient in mind is a key skill that providers need to master in order to be successful in this evolving market—and is also a reason to partner with a health system to achieve and sustain mastery.

Employer-based health insurance allowed patients to become somewhat disconnected from the actual cost of care. This created ever-increasing levels of expenditure on healthcare services without any meaningful way to connect the services provided to demonstrable value or quality for patient's health. By shifting more of the "burden" of paying for healthcare services back to the patient, there is a belief that they will more carefully consider both the need and the timing of care. However, this is a trend that has yet to be fully proven as a viable approach.

In response to all of the changes in employer-based healthcare insurance, many providers have moved to direct care approaches like concierge medicine. In this model, the patient pays a subscription (some would say a premium) directly to the provider to receive expedited and extended care. This approach can work well for certain specialties like pediatrics, primary care, and some others. However, it requires a very entrepreneurial mindset that not every physician has, and it's an approach to care delivery that not every community can or will support. To some this just sounds a lot like the old open access model but now with dollars attached that don't appear to truly add value in the form of improved outcomes or improved patient engagement.

Michael Porter in a 2010 *New England Journal of Medicine* article stated that: "The failures to adopt value as the central goal in healthcare and to measure value are arguably the most serious failures of the medical community." This, he said, has among other things, "resulted in ill-advised cost containment and encouraged micromanagement of physician practices, which imposes significant costs of its own."[3]

Shifting Physician Demographics Are Also Impacting Hospitals and Practices

In the midst of all these shifting dynamics, America's physician supply is undergoing changes as well. One big challenge: Very soon there may not be enough of them. In the spring of 2016 the Association of American Medical Colleges projected "a shortage ranging between 61,700 and 94,700 [by 2025], with a significant shortage showing among many surgical specialties."[4]

The Great Recession of 2008-2009 forestalled the reduction in active providers available to patients (due to retirement delays) but ultimately will not prevent it. As Baby Boomers enter their later years *en masse*, there will be a surge in the demand for care that will need to be accommodated by a shrinking pool of physicians—many of whom are stretched thin, burned out, and disillusioned.

Yet there is also an encouraging countertrend. According to the *New England Journal of Medicine*, "Between 2002 and 2014, a total of 16 new allopathic and 15 new osteopathic medical schools opened in the United States and many existing schools increased their class sizes for an estimated 49 percent increase in first-year enrollment nationwide."[5]

Also, the aforementioned AAMC press release had this to say: "To help alleviate the shortage, the AAMC supports a multipronged solution, which includes innovations in care delivery, better use of technology, and increased federal support for an additional 3,000 new residency positions a year over the next five years. Medical schools have done their part to increase the overall number of physicians by expanding their class sizes, and now Congress must approve a modest increase in federal support for new doctor training if the United States is to increase its overall number of physicians, according to [AAMC President and CEO Darrell G. Kirch, MD]."[6]

Another change is that younger physicians simply don't want to work the same way as their older counterparts. For older physicians, long, intense work weeks were viewed as a necessity, if not a badge of honor. Millennial physicians, in keeping with the attitudes of this cohort overall, seek a healthier, more sustainable work-life blend. (Reinforcing this trend is the fact that, today, there are more women in medical school than there are men.)

These factors, in conjunction with all the others we've touched on, will hugely impact the way hospitals and physician practices are run. Team-based care—with nurse practitioners and physician assistants becoming the frontline care providers—will become more and more prevalent as we move forward. More and more urgent care-type access points will spring up. And telehealth set-ups, where physicians and patients connect via digital data exchange platforms and video chat, will become more widely used and accepted.

None of These Changes Are Easy to Navigate

If all of this feels overwhelming, we understand. There are so many different moving pieces to process and account for that it can easily paralyze even the most gifted leader. And of course, they're already wrestling with some pretty devastating fallout. In most practices there's simply no mechanism in place for leadership training, for supplying physicians with meaningful data, for eliciting a two-way dialogue with them, for holding them accountable. Physicians are crippled by real-time issues that affect quality, efficiency, and ability to care for patients. Not surprisingly, they are frustrated, exhausted, and burned out—all of which create even more problems for leaders.

The good news is that Huron and Studer Group have a long, rich history of helping leaders in healthcare systems and medical practices of all sizes achieve positive change and improve performance. We know what works. We know what doesn't. And we understand how—and just as important, *in what order*—to implement changes so you hardwire them into your culture.

In this book we will discuss how the medical group fits into all the changes we have just overviewed. We will also discuss the crucial role of practice leadership and will lay out a proven framework and a series of evidence-based tactics for aligning, measuring, and developing individual leaders.

We'll teach you how to pinpoint your market, maximize the effectiveness of your governance, and differentiate your practice from the competition. We'll delve into the details of creating a more efficient practice (including overcoming many of the barriers we've just described). We'll offer a roadmap for engaging and retaining all stakeholders, from physicians to staff members to patients to health system partners. And yes, we will tie it all up with a financial primer aimed at ensuring the margin to live the mission.

Finally, we'll include a chapter devoted to academic medical groups, community health centers, and other anomalous practice types. In working with these kinds of organizations, we have learned that they face additional or unique considerations that we believe warrant some increased focus. That's why we have included a chapter to connect this book to them. Yet even without this chapter, we believe the book provides a solid foundation for leaders of these groups and hope that they'll read it from the beginning.

(By the way...don't be thrown by the fact that we use certain terms interchangeably in this book. Specifically, I'm referring to words such as *medical practice, medical group, health system, organization, clinician, physician,* and *provider.* There is a lot of variation in how we think and talk about our industry's institutions and our titles and roles. Our choice to alternate between these words reflects this reality. The same goes for our interchangeable use of "he" and "she." Of course we know there are male *and* female leaders, clinicians, employees, and patients!)

Ultimately, it is our hope that this book will help you respond thoughtfully and well to the long and continual state of change that has wracked healthcare for the past several decades. We are in the middle of the third wave of change. Wave two was centered on the changes in how healthcare is provided, funded, and managed that occurred with HMOs and consolidation in the '90s. Wave one was centered on the creation of health insurance plans and government funding of healthcare in the '60s.

Here's the lesson: In order to stay ahead of the game, both organization leaders and physicians must ride these waves and not try to avoid them. There is no standing still. There are no placid waters. The key is in knowing how to make the right moves at the right time so that, rather than getting overwhelmed and pulled under, you are able to rise to new heights as you seek to live out your mission.

The really good news is that the simple truths still hold. The patient and physician relationship may be changing, but it is not going away. The ability of a physician to diagnose and construct a meaningful treatment plan is still the key to a successful medical practice. We're here to help you do that with as little pain as possible—and with no small measure of anticipation and excitement for the exciting future that's waiting for us all.

CHAPTER 2

Mission, Vision, and Values:
The *Why* Behind Everything We Do

"Vision without action is a daydream. Action without vision
is a nightmare."
—Japanese proverb

Every organization exists for a reason. When we get up every day, brush our
teeth, get dressed, and go to work, we may *think* we're doing it because we
"have to," because we need the paycheck to pay our bills, or (in a few cases)
simply because we need structure for our day and something to fill up our
time. But that's not the whole truth.

Businesses exist because customers want and need the goods and services
they produce—from food to clothing to household appliances to accounting
to pet sitting to pedicures—either to live or to make the living worthwhile.
This is true of factories that churn out cheap plastic cat figurines (*you* might
not value them but someone clearly does). And it's *certainly* true of medical
practices that save lives, promote healing, and keep people well.

So that brings us to *your* organization. There's a reason all the leaders, clinicians, nurses, and other staff members come together every day. They're
here to achieve something very specific. And they've agreed to live by certain
principles while they're working to achieve that "something."

What we're describing here is your mission, vision, and values. These three concepts together represent the heart and soul of everything your medical practice is and does.

We cannot emphasize this enough: Your mission, vision, and values (MVV) must be well thought out, thoroughly understood, and allowed to be the guiding force behind every decision made and every goal set. And they must be communicated regularly so that every member of your team doesn't just "know" them but lives them. Your MVV is the crystallization of the *why* that drives everything you do and say.

When these criteria are not met, "mission, vision, and values" is meaningless corporate speak. When they *are* met, MVV statements become the guideposts by which an organization navigates. Together they say, "This is who we are, why we exist, and the standards we hold ourselves accountable to."

Mission, Vision, and Values at a Glance

MISSION. A written current-state declaration—crafted in clear and concise terminology—that captures who you are, what you do, and who you do it for today. Your current plans, actions, and behaviors should flow from your mission.

VISION. A future-focused statement that describes what an organization plans or hopes to be in the future. This is more of an inspirational or motivational statement that is meant to drive employees and also clearly demonstrate an organization's goals to stakeholders (patients, physicians, staff, etc.).

VALUES. The operating principles and behaviors that guide an organization's internal conduct as well as its relationship with its customers, partners, and shareholders. Values are something that both the organization as a whole as well as each individual team member should be expected to live up to every day.

A group's mission, vision, and values statements are typically developed by its senior leadership in conjunction with its board. Yet they should not be thought of as being fixed or static. From time to time, your MVV statements should be revisited—especially when the practice joins forces with other medical groups or health systems—to make sure they fit the changing world you are operating in.

For example, we once worked with a larger orthopedic surgery practice that also owned its surgery center. While this practice had started out as solely orthopedic surgeons, a few years before they engaged us, they had branched out into other specialties including physiatrists (PM&R) and sports medicine along with adding physical and occupational therapists. So at the time we met them, about half the clinicians were practicing surgeons and the other half were not.

The practice asked us to help them resolve conflicts around how to compensate their equity physician partners regarding profits that included their surgery center and therapy practice sites. So we asked, "What does your mission say?" They said something like, "To be the best orthopedic surgery practice in the world." There was no mention at all of providing care outside of surgery. That's a problem when half of your clinicians aren't surgeons.

What this told us was the practice had not updated its mission, vision, and values in some time. That, in turn, meant it couldn't possibly be eating, sleeping, and breathing its MVV like it should have been. Like many practices, it was coasting along, rudderless, lacking a sharply defined identity. Individual providers were no doubt doing a good job for individual patients—but it couldn't possibly be the powerful, unified, high-performing practice it could have been.

After working with them to update their MVV, it became clear that their mission was to provide great muscular and skeletal care, regardless of the appropriate treatment modality. With this clarity, the equity partners agreed to equally share in the profits from both the surgery center and the therapy practice.

Now, let's talk a little more about each component.

Your MISSION: Who You Are, What You Do, and Most Importantly, *Why* You Do It

Years ago, Matthew, one of the authors of this book, did some work with Changi General Hospital and its multi-specialty medical practice in Singapore. (This was a public health system with 22 medical specialties.) In one of his meetings there, he noticed the following had been chiseled on the wall of the boardroom in marble.

> "To provide a level of patient care and services good enough for our own mothers, without the need for special arrangements."

This is a beautiful example of a mission. It's simple, clear, and very personal. Everyone reading this book knows exactly what it means and immediately applies it to themselves: If my mother got sick and had to see a doctor at my practice, would it be okay for her to call the appointment line like everyone else? Or would I feel compelled to "go around the back" and make sure she gets special treatment?

Basically, Changi is saying, "We plan to treat everyone equally, to give everyone high-quality care, to make everyone feel important and special." And by connecting that thought to one of the most universal figures of love and devotion—mother—it evokes a powerful response. We all have (or had) a mother...and most of us love her fiercely.

Now, your mission doesn't have to literally be chiseled in marble like Changi's is (though it couldn't hurt). But it needs to be so deeply carved into your culture that no one can ever forget it.

If you are looking for guidance for creating (or reworking) your own mission, this book should help you. For example, later chapters will talk about determining what patient segment you are going to serve and how best to create a brand experience for them. Your mission should certainly line up with these decisions.

Your mission drives everything you do. Consider these two samples:

1. "Our goal is to provide comprehensive healthcare to people in our community regardless of their ability to pay."
2. "Our goal is to provide the best orthopedic surgery in the three-state region."

Both of these are fine mission statements but they are very different. They drive very different behavior. They tell you about what kinds of services you should build, what kind of margin you're going after, where you should set up shop, what your practice should look like, and so forth.

Your VISION: Where You Aspire to Go

Here are several vision statements we like:

National Multiple Sclerosis Society: *A world free of multiple sclerosis.*

Make-A-Wish Foundation: *Our vision is that people everywhere will share the power of a wish.*

Kaiser Permanente: *We are trusted partners in total health, collaborating with people to help them thrive and creating communities that are among the healthiest in the nation.*

Leukemia and Lymphoma Society: *To cure leukemia, lymphoma, Hodgkin's disease, and myeloma and improve the quality of life for patients and their families.*

A vision statement is exactly what the word suggests: It's a way to paint a picture for people that they can clearly see in their mind's eye. It's a long-term, end-state vision that every team member can rally behind, be inspired by, aspire to, and enthusiastically pursue even when (especially when) times are tough.

Look at our examples and you'll see that vision statements are bold and ambitious. They're about curing fatal diseases completely (not just "treating" them). They're about becoming "the world's leader" (not the biggest practice in [insert hometown name here]. They reference "people everywhere" (not just "some people").

Visions describe your ultimate end-state. They're not meant to be something you can accomplish tomorrow, this year, or even this decade. Vision statements aren't really about realism; they are about inspiring dreams. They're about motivating people to tirelessly chase after those dreams. They're about giving stressed out, exhausted clinicians and employees a reason to get out of bed in the morning. They should continuously reconnect us to *why* we do what we do and make us aspire to push forward.

Your VALUES: How You Show Your Commitment to Mission

Both of us, Vic and Matthew, work for Huron. Below is a depiction of our company's values.

INTEGRITY
We do the right thing regardless of the consequences.

PURSUIT OF EXCELLENCE
We continually strive to exceed the expectations of our people and our clients.

ACCOUNTABILITY
We take responsibility for individual and collective actions.

COLLABORATION
We work together to achieve collective and individual goals.

PASSION
Our energy and enthusiasm are contagious. We are inspired to make a lasting impact.

Figure 2.1 | Example of Huron's Values

Our leaders make these values meaningful by demonstrating them in action on a daily basis. And to reinforce these values in our culture, we have multiple steps in place to make sure we live and breathe them every day. For example:

- Our mandatory onboarding process introduces our values to every team member and quizzes them on them to confirm core understanding.

- Ongoing employee training reinforces our values and builds on them.
- Our employee recognition programs are all based on one or more of these values. Each award explicitly connects back to the value(s) demonstrated.
- Our performance review and compensation systems specifically review team member performance against these values both to provide positive reinforcement as well as to address any significant transgressions.
- We talk about these values with our prospective clients as part of deciding to work together. And we ask our prospective clients about their values. Ensuring our values will sync with our clients is an important consideration in the work we agree to tackle as a firm.

When communicated regularly and embedded in the culture, values become the DNA of the organization. They serve as the "guardrails" for employee behavior. To borrow one of Huron's values and apply it to a medical group, what might passion look like in action?

Let's say your organization prides itself on being patient-centric. Your mission statement emphasizes that you exist to serve them. So if serving with passion is one of your actions, do you make a point to always be warm, accommodating, and helpful? Or do you make patients feel like they're an intrusion on your day?

Have you or a team member ever said things like, "Let's hurry up with this needle stick. You're the only thing standing between me and lunch!" or, "Only one more hour until quitting time!"? Have you or a team member ever made a patient stand waiting for five minutes while you finished up a phone call with a colleague in another location?

These are *not* obvious black and white transgressions—in fact, statements like the first two are usually made in a lighthearted fashion. They're certainly not malicious. But they are the kinds of statements that make patients feel, at least on a subconscious level, that you are not passionate about serving them. And when patients have to wait until you finish your phone call—even if it's a work-related call and not a chat with your spouse or best friend—they may feel the same way.

Do you really live your values? Let's say one of your practice's values is teamwork. Do you adjust call schedules to support team members at different points in their life when they need a little extra help (such as when an employee has a sick baby or a death in the family)? If you have a value of equality—everyone's job is important and everyone has a voice—how does your staff interact in the hallway? Do leaders, clinicians, and employees treat people as if there are different "classes" on your team?

One of our leaders has a plaque in her office that reads, "Do your values hang on the wall or do they walk in the hall?" Most of us have probably heard variations of this adage elsewhere, but there's something about seeing it there every week that serves as a very powerful reminder.

Ensuring Practice-Wide Alignment to Mission, Vision, and Values

Is *everyone* on your team aligned with the mission, vision, and values of your practice? The willingness to live MVV should be "table stakes" for working at your practice. People, as individuals, need to feel responsible for upholding them every day and holding their colleagues accountable.

If you're an OB practice, for instance, you might expect small children to accompany moms to their appointments. Hopefully, family friendliness is part of your mission and vision. That means every employee should feel personally responsible for creating that feeling. No staff member should ever use language that wouldn't be appropriate in front of children—but you might be surprised by how often it happens. (We've witnessed a physician literally using curse words with a staff member behind the reception desk where families and small children could hear her.)

So how do you ensure that mission, vision, and values become an inherent part of the fabric of your practice? You focus on them, verbally and in writing, over and over again every chance you have and in as many ways as possible. Here are a few tips you can implement:

Embed MVV into your standards of behavior. These documents contain specific guidelines that spell out the expectations you have for leaders, clinicians, and employees. These guidelines are *very* specific—they can include a statement like "Don't use curse words with fellow team members"—if need be. Every employee signs a copy to show that they are committed to living up to your mission, vision, and values. (To learn more about standards of behavior and how to implement them in your organization, visit www.studergroup. com/medical-group/standards-of-behavior.)

Emphasize them during recruiting. Be crystal clear with potential new hires that this is why you exist (mission), this is where you see yourself going (vision), and this is how team members are expected to behave (values). We actually give job candidates a copy of our standards of behavior to sign before they ever proceed with an interview. Perhaps 5 percent of our candidates choose not to return the signed document to us. This is a good thing, as it allows us to quickly screen-out poor matches for our culture: These people are telling us, up front, that they don't agree to live by our MVV. Therefore they are not candidates we should consider.

Talk more about them during the onboarding process. Not only should you train people on what they'll be expected to do on the job, you'll explain why you expect them to do so. "Our mission references creating a positive experience for patients and families, so we lead mothers with young children over to the children's corner of our waiting area. We point out the books and show patients how to use the remote control to change the channel."

Open key strategic meetings throughout the year with a refresher course on MVV. This reminds leaders of the *why* so they'll stay within these guidelines when strategizing a new direction or hammering out new initiatives for the company.

Teach leaders to connect back to mission, vision, and values when they introduce and train on a new initiative. It will greatly increase buy-in from clinicians and staff when leaders speak to their sense of purpose and remind them of the meaning behind their work.

Reward and recognize high performance that's linked to MVV. Whether you're offering a monetary bonus for exceeding a goal, giving an award, or publicly praising an employee, be sure to connect what the team member did to your organization's larger purpose. How did he fulfill your mission? Promote your vision? Demonstrate your values?

Capture and share organizational stories to embed them firmly into your culture. Leaders should actively seek out, capture, and share great examples of team members demonstrating your MVV. It's one thing to say you are "patient-centric"; it's quite another to share the example of the clinician who made a house call on the way home because the patient was unable to arrange transportation to the clinic for an urgent need.

By doing the hard work of clarifying your mission, vision, and values and weaving it into the fabric of your culture, you're making the rest of the tasks laid out in this book much easier. People need a sense of purpose if they're to put their heart into their work. When you help them define that purpose and its parameters, you go a long way toward helping them find the energy, motivation, and passion to move toward excellence.

CHAPTER 3

The Critical Role of Leadership— From Vision to Reality

"If your actions inspire others to dream more, learn more, do more, and become more, you are a leader."
—John Quincy Adams

"Leaders are made; they are not born. They are made by hard effort, which is the price all of us must pay to achieve any goal that is worthwhile."
—Vince Lombardi

Please take a moment to consider the team of highly skilled specialists it takes to build a house. Architects, excavators, framers, electricians, plumbers, cabinetmakers, electricians, flooring installers—all play a vital role in the construction process. The house can't come together without them. Yet these critical players won't be able do their work at the right times and in the right sequence without *another* highly skilled professional directing and coordinating them.

The same is true of a medical practice. A well-trained "village" of physicians, physician assistants, nurse practitioners, nurses, medical assistants, lab workers, front desk staff, and other experts come together to care for patients—but someone has to be running the show.

In construction that point person is the general contractor. In our particular corner of healthcare it's the practice leader—or *leaders* as the case may be.

As medical groups relentlessly grow bigger and more complicated, so does the job of leading them. In the same way that building a small cottage is easier than building a sprawling multi-floor high rise, it's easier to manage 20 healthcare professionals than to manage 200—and certainly 2,000.

The person who successfully ran a modestly sized practice ten years ago probably can't keep up with today's much bigger version—not without a lot of training, anyway. It takes far more leadership muscle to run the complex, integrated, ever-expanding medical groups that are quickly becoming the new normal.

Yes, the healthcare industry is changing—rapidly and drastically—and that means the role of leadership is more critical than ever. Great leaders are needed to usher us through the great transformation that we're all experiencing. In fact, they are the change agents.

You may remember from science class that entropy is the default process of the Universe. Things naturally devolve from order to chaos unless some force intervenes. If any medical group has a prayer of evolving to fit the future we discussed in Chapter 1 (rather than succumbing to entropy), leaders must be that force.

By the way...we'd like to take this moment to clarify that we view and will refer to leadership and management as the same thing. The notion that you can separate them just doesn't work in real life. So when we use the term "leadership" throughout this book, know that if your job involves inspiring, motivating, or guiding people in any way, we're talking to you.

The Leader's REAL Job: Helping People Remember the *Why*

When you're a leader, your number one job is to get the organization connected back to its *why*—as expressed by the Mission, Vision, and Values we discussed in the previous chapter. You need to bring these concepts to life every day, to make them more than words on a wall. You'll need to help your team members remember exactly why they chose the work they do—and why they must strive to do it better and better every day.

And since very few (if any) organizations are "there" yet in terms of perfectly fulfilling their Mission, Vision, and Values statements, it's up to you to make people see that the changes they're being asked to make will get the results that matter (and that create the momentum to keep change rolling forward).

Jim Collins, author of *Good to Great*, famously said that successful change happens via the "flywheel effect." Leaders slowly and consistently begin turning the flywheel, all the while providing evidence that what they're asking their employees to do will get results. Eventually, momentum takes over, and change accelerates as people gain confidence from seeing the successes unfold.[1]

Studer Group's version of this model, the Healthcare Flywheel®, adapts this to healthcare. At the "hub" of the flywheel are the words "purpose, worthwhile work, and making a difference"—which represent the inherent core values that drive healthcare professionals. And around this core axle you will find the prescriptive to-dos, bottom-line results, and self-motivation that keep the wheel turning.

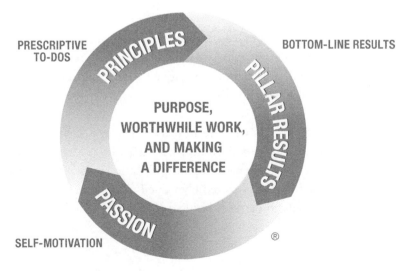

Figure 3.1 | The Healthcare Flywheel®

It's up to us as leaders to consistently help clinicians, nurses, and other team members connect back to these core values. Reminding them how the dry metrics you're aiming for connect to what matters—a healthy new baby, the smile of a child when the cast comes off, the grandma who finally gets her diabetes under control—gets people excited and engaged. This causes them to do more of what generated those results. This, in turn, leads to even better results. And so on.

If you are a leader, getting this flywheel turning is your real job. Sure, there are certain foundational skills you must be able to do—holding performance reviews, running effective meetings, managing financial resources, hiring (and firing) employees, etc.—but it's the ability to connect people back to their passion and purpose that truly makes a leader a leader.

Building a Successful Leadership Team: Five Factors That Make the Difference

> "In fact, leaders of companies that go from good to great start not with 'where' but with 'who.' They start by getting the right people on the bus, the wrong people off the bus, and the right people in the right seats. And they stick with that discipline—first the people, then the direction—no matter how dire the circumstances."
> —Jim Collins, Good to Great

What does this Collins quote mean for the medical group that's struggling to stay upright as an industry shifts beneath its feet? It boils down to this: *Invest in your leaders.* Hire the right people, give them clear goals to strive for, incentivize them to meet those goals.

Don't just assume the leaders who are in place right now—who've been in place perhaps for many years—will somehow, magically, rise to the occasion just because the practice really needs them to. While the practice manager of a three-physician group is an incredibly valued member of the team, that doesn't mean he is ready to be the administrative leader of a 300-physician group.

In healthcare we tend to rearrange the people we have and create the roles around them. It should be the other way around. Form should follow function. We should create the roles the organization needs and then put the right people in them. (An easy litmus test for making sure you're not creating a role for a specific employee is to ask yourself: *If this person were to quit tomorrow, would I replace them?* If not, you have to ask yourself why you put them in that job in the first place.)

To address the other part of Collins's quote, if you have the wrong people on your bus, you need to do the hard work of getting them off the bus—if not off altogether, then at least out of the wrong seats and into the right ones. Yes, it's tough. But leaders who shouldn't be leaders can hold a medical practice back from living up to its full potential.

SUCCESS FACTOR 1: Smart Leadership Selection. There are various key leadership roles inside a medical practice. In our chapter on governance we identify some of the most common ones and outline the responsibilities that come with them. Our point here, however, is simple: Whatever leadership position you're seeking to fill, be intentional about who you hire.

Historically, the first doctor who established a medical practice would end up running the place. All the others would become his junior partners. The problem—even beyond the sheer size that most practices have grown to—is that the person who is good at running a solo shop is usually *not* good at running a group. This is not just a healthcare thing: Whatever the industry, entrepreneurs tend not to make great CEOs. The two roles require different skill sets.

When hiring a leader, you want to select for skill, experience, and cultural fit. Often organizations look only internally because they think it will take too long for an outsider to learn how they work. But if you're looking to transform the culture of your practice, promoting from within is a mistake. How can you expect somebody who created the culture you have today to be the change agent for the culture you want tomorrow? You can't.

Should I Hire a Senior Leader from Within...Or Look Outside the Organization?

Do you love your culture? If you do, hire your president or senior leader from within. If you don't—if you're looking for your culture to transform—look outside your organization. It really is a simple question but it's one that many groups don't consider when they are ready to fill this (or another) crucial role.

We once worked with a health system that made the mistake of promoting a medical group CEO from within. They felt that it would take an outsider too long to get up to speed, so they selected a department chair who had been inside the organization for 10 years. He knew all the players. He knew how to navigate the politics. He knew how to reduce conflict and create calm. What he *didn't* know how to do was make transformative leadership decisions.

In short, this health system needed a change agent, but they hired a peacemaker.

If you need someone to come in and shake up the culture of your medical group, it's probably best to look externally. Don't get too hung up on how long the transition will take. Yes, it takes six months for an outsider to get up to speed—but it also takes six months for an insider to get used to the fact that she's not in her old role but in a new one. In other words, it's a wash.

Keep other factors in mind as well. If you always hire *internally*, you will miss out on some great talent. If you always hire *externally*, high performers in your organization may not feel they have career opportunities—and therefore you might not be able to retain your high performers. It's a sticky issue. Give the decision the careful attention it deserves and be prepared to explain *why* you made the decision you did.

When hiring a leader at any level, peer interviewing is crucial. Essentially, this means asking team members to participate in the hiring process. Leaders identify high and solid performers to interview their future peers. These employees are trained by human resources on how to interview to avoid any legal issues. Then, leaders deploy them to interview only candidates they (the leaders) have screened and feel are worth consideration.

This process helps ensure that the cultural fit is right. Plus, it gets people invested in the new hire's success—i.e., "We helped hire this person so we are accountable for helping him be successful."

When we recommend peer interviewing, we hear two main objections. The first one is, "Peer interviewing takes too long." To that we reply, "It's better to take your time and hire the right person than to hire the wrong person and spend the next six months figuring out how to get rid of him."

The other objection we hear is, "But what if peers end up blackballing someone I really wanted to hire?" We find the answer to this one is a question: "Are you choosing the person you're choosing for the right reasons?" Healthcare is a team sport. If the team rejects a player, the team won't be happy and the player won't be successful. In other words, don't hire the orthopedic surgeon who doesn't play well with others or the nurse with the bad attitude. You'll get massive pushback, and no one will win.

What should leaders and peers look for when interviewing candidates? We like to take a cue from Warren Buffett, who has been quoted as saying:

> *"Somebody once said that in looking for people to hire, you look for three qualities: integrity, intelligence, and energy. And if you don't have the first, the other two will kill you. You think about it; it's true. If you hire somebody without [integrity], you really want them to be dumb and lazy."*

How can you best ascertain these Buffett-approved qualities as part of interviewing? We recommend using behavioral-based interviewing questions.

The premise behind behavioral-based interviewing is that our past actions are most likely to define how we will behave in the future.

Behavioral-based interviewing questions are open-ended questions that ask things about past decisions, outcomes, and learnings. Here are some examples:

- Tell me about a time you were unable to meet a deadline, how you handled it, and what you do differently now as a result of this.
- Tell me about a time you were juggling multiple high-importance priorities. How did you go about prioritizing them and what outcome did you experience?
- Can you share with me an example of when you had to treat a patient whose personal beliefs you strongly disagreed with? How did you go about providing them with high-quality care despite your personal beliefs? How did it turn out?

You can learn more about peer interviewing and behavioral-based interviewing on Studer Group's website at www.studergroup.com/medical-group/peer-interviewing.

SUCCESS FACTOR 2: Shared and Aligned Goals. In a nutshell, your leaders' goals need to be aligned with the overall goals of the organization and shared with other relevant cross-functional leaders. We'll discuss this subject more in-depth in Chapter 4. But for now, consider the analogy of an Olympic rowing team. If everyone isn't rowing in same direction, there is no way the team can be successful.

At first glance this feels like an overly simplistic truism. Yet when you look at the reality inside most groups, you'll find people aren't rowing in harmony. Most leaders get the shared vision, "We want to be the best medical practice in this region of the country." What they *don't* get is how to answer the question, "What does that mean in terms of this year's goals?" Be the best at what? Are we trying to become number one in *everything*? Or are we trying to move from the 20th percentile to the 50th on a specific metric?

Achieving goals requires sharing them—not just with leaders but also with staff. Yet we find that some organizations keep such goals confidential, sometimes due to the advice of an attorney. In such cases, listening to the attorney is probably a mistake. People don't need to know a leader's salary, but they do need to know what she is trying to achieve. How else can they help the leader meet her goals?

Lack of transparency is only one of the big roadblocks to meeting leader goals. Another one is too many priorities. When everything is a priority, nothing is a priority. Too many initiatives create a lot of "flailing" as they compete for leader attention, yet despite all the noise and chaos nothing actually gets better. (In fact, it usually gets worse.)

This is why we recommend practices use the Leader Evaluation Manager® tool—it forces them to give each goal a weight to prioritize them. Again, we'll cover this topic in more detail in the next chapter.

SUCCESS FACTOR 3: Shared Clear Responsibilities. Successful leadership teams know who is responsible for what. Who is in charge of scheduling? Billing? Patient complaints? Hiring and firing staff? Setting policy? When responsibilities aren't clearly defined and known by everyone, counterproductive or even destructive patterns usually emerge. Worse, no one stops them.

One day we were in a clinic affiliated with one of our clients, and the phone rang a couple of times. A pediatrician got aggravated and berated the staff, "You let that phone ring! We don't allow phones to ring here!" Then, when he left the room, one staff member leaned over and told a new team member, "Oh, I should have told you. When that doctor is on duty we all just turn our phone ringers off so he won't yell at us."

Should this really be happening? Is it really that physician's place to set and enforce a phone policy of turning off the phone ringers? Of course not. Failing to answer phone calls is not good practice! But when we investigated, we discovered no one had ever said to the physician, "Hey, Doctor, it's important that we can hear the phones ring so we can answer them. We know they can be annoying to hear at times, but sending every call to voicemail is not a good option." Further, we learned that when our client acquired the physician practice years ago, this particular physician had been squelching the phone for more than a decade. That's just the way it was; nobody wanted to do anything about it. And so nothing changed.

Here's another example of what can spring up inside a "responsibility vacuum." We worked with a large health system that had an OB practice and a pediatrics practice in the same building. Yet, even though they served the same patients and had the same system logo on the door, they had completely different advance practice professional policies. One required patients to sign, acknowledging that they received the policy, while the other provided a different policy and didn't ask for a signature.

This left their shared patients to wonder, *What's so different about the nurse practitioner in the OB practice versus the one in the pediatrics practice that they have different policies?* It was confusing, at best. And this is a health system that aspires to be patient-centric. Yet when we asked the clinic leaders who was responsible for reconciling the APP process, no one knew.

SUCCESS FACTOR 4: Consistent Execution. What does good leadership actually look like? It manifests as *consistency*. People want to know what to expect from their leaders. In fact, a Google study found the quality employees value most in a leader is *predictability*. They value it even over brilliance, academic credentials, and other criteria that may seem more exciting.[2]

Leadership consistency doesn't happen by accident. When we want to create a high-reliability organization—one where everything happens the same way from the check-in process to the forms given to patients to how insurance information is disclosed—we put rules in place and deliberately and methodically follow them. Right? Well, high-reliability leadership occurs when we develop leaders in the same unified way.

Leader behavior must be *aligned*. How a leader deals with a disruptive employee, for example, should be the same in Clinic A as it is in Clinic B. People need (and want) to know what is expected of them. They need (and want) to know that the rules don't change based on which doctor or which clinic manager is working that day. After all, if leaders are not role modeling consistency, how can we expect staff to demonstrate consistency in delivering reliable care to patients?

Also, leaders at all levels must be held *accountable* for following established processes and procedures. When people become leaders, we as an industry often stop validating their actions. This is a mistake. If an organization rolls out AIDET®—Studer Group's patient communication framework whose acronym stands for **A**cknowledge, **I**ntroduce, **D**uration, **E**xplanation, and **T**hank You—leaders must set the example. If they don't adhere to initiatives and uphold standards, neither will the people below them.

Whether or not leaders execute consistently boils down to the old "skill vs. will" debate. If you've established what an organizational skill looks like and trained leaders in how to do it, and they're still executing poorly, it's a *will* issue. If you're not sure you've done a good job of training them, it's time to take a look at your development practices and focus on the skill. In general, we recommend you give people the benefit of the doubt and start by assuming they have a skill gap. Then, only after providing them training opportunities should you assume it's a will problem.

SUCCESS FACTOR 5: Leadership Development. No doubt about it: Leadership skills are worth investing in. This is true for both physician and administrative leaders. Consider the impact of fundamental leader skills— for instance, the ability to hold an effective annual review, for instance. Done well, these reviews improve performance and create loyalty. Done poorly, they can cause people to leave.

Don't mistake management training for leadership development. MBAs are wonderful skill builders, but the skills they build are theoretical. There is a big difference between reading about a skill in a textbook or watching it on YouTube and actually doing it. This is why in medicine doctors follow the "see one, do one, teach one" philosophy.

The same is true of leadership development. Leaders need to see what right looks like, they need to practice it with a feedback loop, then ultimately (after they've developed the skill) they need to be able to teach it to the next generation. And this type of skill building *cannot* happen with a one-time training event.

We recommend our partner organizations hold one- to two-day Leadership Development Institutes (LDIs) once a quarter. Basically, these are regularly scheduled sessions in which a leadership team comes together for intensive training focused on skills that have been identified as needing improvement to meet organizational goals.

This may seem like a lot. After all, for doctors being paid on RVUs, those days of training represent a fair amount of lost revenue. Yet when you understand the financial impact of the skills their leaders are learning, you'll come to see that the investment is worth it. Think of it this way: What does it cost a practice to have 30 percent annualized staff turnover? What does it cost to have two more physicians a year quit the practice than would quit if you'd had better leadership in place?

Our advice is two-fold. One, don't make the training theoretical. Don't choose a popular leadership book and focus on a chapter a month. (Yes, this happens more than it should and it's almost always a waste of time.) Two, tailor the training to needs/problems your organization is currently facing. Make sure sessions are immediately relevant and can be put into practice by your leaders.

For example, if you're struggling to hit a revenue goal, then leadership development should be focused on the skills to address that. One practice we worked with was struggling with patient access. So our leadership sessions brought physician and administrative leadership together to focus on building and developing their skills to drive better access.

We helped them ask relevant questions like: Should we address the hours we're open? Should we address schedule availability? Have we standardized our scheduling templates to support more open access? Are there ways to better leverage the advanced practice providers to be able to accommodate last-minute requests? Do we need to simplify our appointment times (i.e., instead of saying we see new patients only in certain time slots, could we find a way to accommodate new patients in *any* slot during the day)?

When you think about leadership training this way, you see that it's an opportunity to address the key operational and leadership issues that need to be improved in your organization.

A Word About Dyad Leadership

Before we close this chapter, we'd like to briefly discuss the concept of dyad leadership. Basically, this is a leadership structure in which administration and medical staff are equally represented in decision making—where "suit coats" and "white coats" join forces to create a better medical group. Dyad leadership may exist at multiple levels throughout the organization:

- The CMO and COO of the health system
- The executive medical director and the chief administrative officer of the medical group
- The chief of surgery and nurse manager of perioperative services in a hospital
- The clinic medical director and clinic manager of an individual clinic

A successful dyad is a lot like a great marriage. Both parties—the physician leader (the "white coat") and the administrative leader (the "suit coat")—bring valuable assets to the table. They complement each other. The key to medical group harmony, like marital harmony, is to know who is accountable for what.

Figure 3.2 | Clear Responsibilities for a Dyad Leadership Model

The goal of dyad leadership is to create a group of physicians and staff where all efforts align with group goals, where behaviors deliver performance, where skills are continuously improving, where there's better-informed problem solving, and where work is energizing and fulfilling. (Not a bad set of conditions!)

Also, the presence of effective dyad leadership greatly reduces the "we/they" problem. In other words, it makes it less likely that employees will seek out the leader they feel is most likely to give them the answer they want to hear. (We like to compare this to the kind of co-parenting that happens when Mom and Dad aren't on the same page; children play one parent against another.)

Dyad leadership allows for greater trust, smoother teamwork, more peer-to-peer support, and the blending of different strengths that come to the table to create long-term success. It's rare, after all, that an administrative leader is also an expert in clinical decision making and processes. This is a model of leadership that tends to foster engagement among employees and clinicians as well as improve recruitment and retention.

"The delivery of medical care is a business; caring for patients is not. A principal goal of the dyad is the effective management of this tension for the good of the patient and the organization."[3]
—Mayo Clinic

"Our management approach relies upon a dyad leadership structure that pairs a physician executive leader with a management executive...We believe the dyad structure promotes teamwork and alignment on culture, strategy, goals, and execution."[4]
—Kaiser Permanente

These are the "pros" of dyad leadership. When such partnerships work, the results can be pretty great. However, they don't always work as intended. Sometimes an organization might be a dyad in name only; one person makes all the decisions and the other simply has an impressive-sounding title and doesn't do much of anything.

Worse than an ineffective dyad is a toxic dyad. Not only might such a partnership not make the team stronger, it might make it weaker. People may divide into two camps with staff members undermining each other. They end up jockeying for power and trying to determine which leader to suck up to.

It's no exaggeration to say that a poorly performing dyad can kill a practice.

Consistency is key to making dyads work. To reference the parenting analogy again, Mom and Dad need to know their roles and be consistent with their expectations and answers within those roles. If Mom says, "No, you can't have a cookie," Dad won't give in to the begging. Why? Because he knows Mom is in charge of cookie allocation. This is why, as we said earlier, it's so crucial for any practice to invest in hiring the right leaders and developing them consistently and well, whether they follow the dyad model or not.

(It's worth noting here that there are some medical groups in which nursing clinical skills are a vital component. They have expanded the dyad model into a triad model that includes traditional administrative and nurse leaders working effectively together.)

Evidence-Based Leadership: A Framework That Drives High Performance

However you structure your medical group, you may find Studer Group's Evidence-Based Leadership^{SM} methodology helpful for developing leaders in a way that meets the criteria we describe in this book and also drives your desired outcomes. Here is a brief overview of the framework.

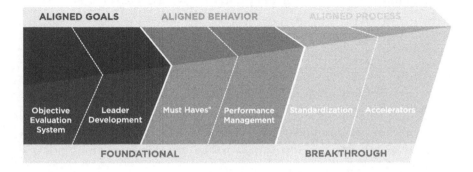

Figure 3.3 | Evidence-Based Leadership® Framework

- **OBJECTIVE EVALUATION SYSTEM:** Implement an organization-wide leadership evaluation system to hardwire objective accountability.
- **LEADER DEVELOPMENT:** Create processes to invest in your leaders' skill building. It is crucial that they develop the leadership competencies necessary to attain desired results.
- **MUST HAVES®:** Hardwire key behaviors across your organization to drive focus. These may include: Rounding, Reward & Recognition, Clinician/Employee Selection, Pre- and Post-Visit Communication, and Key Words at Key Times/AIDET.
- **PERFORMANCE MANAGEMENT:** Re-recruit high and middle performers, move low performers up or out, and hold team members accountable to organization-wide standards of conduct.
- **STANDARDIZATION:** Establish standards for how you operate and create consistency within your organization. Examples of

standardization may include: agendas by pillar, peer interviewing, 30/90-day sessions, and organizational dashboards.

- **ACCELERATORS:** These are software solutions designed to support and accelerate your efforts to hardwire the Evidence-Based Leadership^{SM} framework. Accelerators include: Leader Evaluation Manager®, Validation Matrix^{SM}, Provider Feedback System^{SM}, MyRounding®, and Patient Call Manager^{SM}.

To learn more about Evidence-Based Leadership and how it works, we recommend that you read *A Culture of High Performance* by Quint Studer. It lays out the framework, principles, processes, and tactics that hardwire excellence in an organization. To learn more about this book, please visit www.firestarterpublishing.com/acultureofhighperformance. You might also visit www.studergroup.com/evidence-based-leadership.

Remember, leadership is a journey, not a destination. It takes time to get any new structure, or any new development initiative, up and running. But if you stick it out, it gets easier. High-performing teams may initially regress—in the same way that couples fight a lot in the first year of marriage as they adjust to the new "rules"—but eventually the partnership gets stronger. In the end, everyone will be glad that you made the effort.

CHAPTER 4

The Management Operating System:
A Framework for Alignment and Accountability

"You can't talk about leadership without talking about responsibility and accountability...you can't separate the two. A leader must delegate responsibility and provide the freedom to make decisions, and then be held accountable for the results."
—Baseball great Buck Rodgers

It's not easy being a physician these days. If you've been practicing medicine for a while, the changes that have wracked the healthcare industry can be a bitter pill indeed. After all, as a doctor, you were master of your domain once upon a time. If you didn't own the practice, you were at least able to set your own schedule, work the way you wanted to work, make your own clinical decisions. It was a simpler, more gratifying time—and for many doctors, it felt like a more lucrative time as well.

Also, let's face it: Life was easier for administrative leaders as well. You were hired and fired by the doctors and worked to serve them. Money was flowing more freely back then, and it probably wasn't a big deal if you fell short on one of your goals (maybe even all of them). As long as the doctors liked you, you probably weren't in danger of losing your job.

Now, all of this has changed. Doctors, other clinicians, and practice administrators have suddenly become employees of some large organization or another (or at least are affiliated with and accountable to one). Now, after many years of relative freedom, they're all being charged with meeting very specific goals, financial and otherwise. And typically the practice group they work for lacks the structure and processes needed to make all these incredibly complicated changes happen—and happen consistently.

We don't have to tell you how daunting these challenges are. Leaders must now manage hundreds, if not thousands, of highly skilled, highly trained professionals who have spent much of their lives doing things in a very different way. And doctors and other clinicians themselves must learn to think like team members rather than individual contributors.

This is not optional, by the way: Physicians must actually *be* team members. While most no longer have the sole decision-making control they once did, they absolutely *cannot* be left out (or allowed to opt out) of the relentless march toward excellence. They bring so much to the table—industry experience, the ability to optimize systems and processes, the ability (and inclination) to be patient advocates, not to mention the fact that they diagnose and direct clinical treatment—that trying to move forward without their full participation would be foolish.

Part of the challenge may be getting physicians fully engaged in the push to reinvent your practice. We'll address this subject (engagement) in Chapter 9. The other part is creating and installing a new management operating system—one that lets physicians and other leaders know exactly what they need to do and holds them accountable for getting it done.

Taking It One Step at a Time

It's no exaggeration that we must totally transform the way medical practices have historically been run. But of course we can't say, "Okay, leader, change the way you do everything, and by the way, here are 43 quality metrics you have to meet by the end of the year. Now *go!*" Human beings don't—*can't*—work this way.

What we *can* do is focus in on one or two pivotal changes at a time. Not only will the metrics directly associated with those changes improve, other metrics that are indirectly connected to them will improve as well.

In the same way that achieving a healthy body weight decreases the likelihood of heart disease, diabetes, and cancer, there are certain predictable, proven changes practices can make that not only solve the problem they're targeting but other ones as well.

One big reason incremental changes work is that they allow people to see that they *can* change things for the better. As they achieve early successes, their confidence builds, momentum surges, and they find themselves emotionally ready to tackle the next metric. This is the Healthcare Flywheel® in action.

To explain this in clinician terms, let's say you are treating an overweight, borderline diabetic patient who needs to lose weight, overhaul her diet, start exercising, and sleep more hours. When taken all together, this is an almost insurmountable set of goals. It's highly unlikely that the patient can make every change she needs to make all at once. Ask her to and she will surely fail, lose confidence, and give up.

What *does* work is asking the patient to focus on one behavior at a time. Perhaps she starts by walking her dog three or four times a week for 20 minutes. After she does that for a month and is well on the way to making walking her dog an engrained habit, she can add a new behavior: say, getting to bed by 10 p.m. so she can get enough sleep. And so forth.

This is how medical practices should think about implementing the many, many changes they need to make in order to stay financially viable. If leaders, clinicians, and staff are able to collectively tackle one behavior a quarter, they can begin to make serious progress.

Goal Setting for Alignment

Goal setting is job one. All goals must be objective, measurable, and aligned across the entire organization. The process begins with the larger health system's high-level goals, which are created at the very top of the organization and stem directly from the mission. For example, if a health system is a non-profit organization, an overall goal might be to financially break even or perhaps to generate a certain amount of margin toward a rainy day fund for the future.

The larger health system's goals then are cascaded to the medical practice CEO's goals. Specifically in this example, a goal would be set to reflect the medical practice's intended financial contribution to the health system. Then the goals would continue to be cascaded to other leaders and when appropriate eventually to individual clinicians. For example, we often ask individual clinicians to achieve specific productivity targets in order for the practice to achieve its overall financial goals.

The purpose of the goal cascade is *alignment*. Each leader and clinician should know what he is responsible for and how his individual performance relates to the larger health system's big picture.

Frankly, goal alignment is one of the biggest challenges we see in our work. The way health systems and medical groups pay clinical and administrative leaders is sometimes inconsistent with the larger organizational goals they've set. When goals are not aligned in this way, leaders can't work together for the greater good of the practice and the health system. What's more, you may have certain leaders winning at the expense of others. Obviously, this works against morale and ultimately causes the "losers" to disengage and perhaps leave for greener pastures.

Consider the following table. The first two columns show what can happen when goals are misaligned. Either the clinician wins, and the practice administrator loses, or vice versa—regardless of the fact that both worked hard and "deserve" a bonus. The third column shows what happens when goals *are* aligned: The organization wins and both parties are recognized for their contribution.

	Goals Not Aligned		**Goals Aligned**
CLINICIAN	* Worked hard * Missed RVU target due to office inefficiencies and new EHR	* Worked hard * Exceeded RVU target by seeing 40+ patients a day on clinic days	* Worked hard * Exceeded RVU target by seeing 40+ patients a day on clinic days
PRACTICE ADMINISTRATOR	* Worked hard * Cut staff expenses and exceeded budget	* Worked hard * Paid overtime to support high-volume clinic days and therefore missed budget	* Worked hard * Achieved financial goals as budget was designed to flex based on RVU productivity
OUTCOME	* Clinician got a poor review and no bonus * Practice administrator got a good review and bonus	* Clinician got a good review and a bonus * Practice administrator got a poor review and no bonus	* Clinician got a good review and a bonus * Practice administrator got a good review and bonus

Figure 4.1 | Example of How Misaligned and Aligned Goals Can Impact Both Clinician and Practice Administrator

Our work with health systems across the country has shown us that there are dozens, if not hundreds, of goals that *could* be placed on leader evaluations. Such a barrage of goals would not be manageable. Typically, they are narrowed down to five to eight metrics the organization wants to achieve in a given performance period. These goals become the key drivers, and from them, subset goals cascade through the leadership hierarchy.

The following example shows how an organization's high-level goals might be aligned and cascaded to the primary care practices. In this example we have focused on a single quality goal and a single financial goal for simplicity.

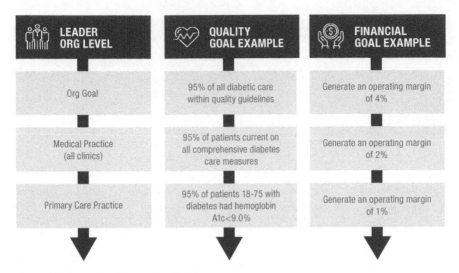

Figure 4.2 | Example of Cascading Goals

You will notice that leaders do not have exactly the same goal at every organizational level. Rather, alignment means that each leader's goal supports the goal of the leader above him and represents his contribution. For an illustration of how this works, see the financial goal above. While the health system has targeted an overall operating margin of 4 percent, the medical practice is aiming to contribute 2 percent and primary care just 1 percent in operating margin. If we were to look at how this goal cascaded to other leaders, we would clearly find some areas that are being asked to contribute higher than a 4 percent operating margin to net out and allow the health system to achieve its goal.

We find most leaders perform best when they are assigned five to eight goals to focus on. Yet even narrowed down this far, leaders can't (and shouldn't) give all of the goals equal focus and effort.

Goals need to be weighted so that people know *exactly* what they will be evaluated (and ultimately compensated) on. We recommend no goal be weighted less than 10 percent. A typical rule of thumb for weighting is as follows:

10 percent equals *awareness*
20 percent equals *focus*
30 percent equals *urgency*

Here is an example of how goals might be weighted for a primary care practice's executive leader. By reviewing these goals, it is easy to quickly note her areas of focus and her priorities. It is important to note that when all the goals are added together the total weight should equal 100 percent (no more and no less).

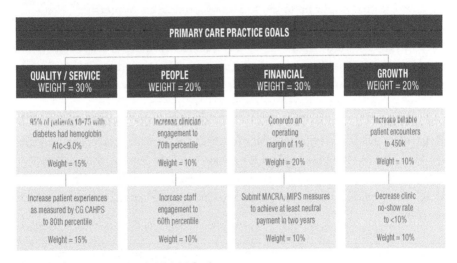

PRIMARY CARE PRACTICE GOALS

QUALITY / SERVICE WEIGHT = 30%	PEOPLE WEIGHT = 20%	FINANCIAL WEIGHT = 30%	GROWTH WEIGHT = 20%
95% of patients 18-75 with diabetes had hemoglobin A1c<9.0% Weight = 15%	Increase clinician engagement to 70th percentile Weight = 10%	Generate an operating margin of 1% Weight = 20%	Increase billable patient encounters to 450k Weight = 10%
Increase patient experiences as measured by CG CAHPS to 80th percentile Weight = 15%	Increase staff engagement to 60th percentile Weight = 10%	Submit MACRA, MIPS measures to achieve at least neutral payment in two years Weight = 10%	Decrease clinic no-show rate to <10% Weight = 10%

Figure 4.3 | Example of How to Weight Goals

To learn more about goal cascading, we invite you to read *A Culture of High Performance: Achieving Higher Quality at a Lower Cost* by Quint Studer. To learn more about this book, please visit www.firestarterpublishing.com/acultureofhighperformance.

By the way, Studer Group® has a software-supported framework called Leader Evaluation Manager® (LEM for short) designed to help organizations—including medical practice leaders—manage all these components. It helps leaders understand the key items they are accountable for achieving and which of those take priority. Even if you don't use LEM it makes sense to structure and cascade your goal setting this way.

To learn more about LEM, please visit www.studergroup.com/how-we-help/healthcare-software-accelerators/leader-evaluation-manager.

Making Goals Doable

So let's say your practice starts with objective goals like those shown in the previous graphics. How do you make sure leaders can achieve them? We recommend breaking that annual goal down into 90-day chunks. (In fact, we have a 90-Day Plan tool that helps facilitate this process.) So if a clinic's goal is to have 200,000 billable encounters during the fiscal year, then in the first 90 days the goal might be to get to 50,000 billable encounters.

Of course, time frames can't always be that cleanly divided. Sometimes there might be a seasonality factor—such as a practice that does a lot of sports physicals or flu shots, for example—in which case the leader might need to achieve more in some quarters than in others in order to hit the annual goal.

Regardless, it's important for senior leaders to stay in the loop regarding their leaders' progress toward goals. Don't wait until the end of the year and say, "Well, how did you do on improving clinical quality?" In fact, we recommend that every leader review goal progress with his immediate supervisor every month.

Studer Group has found that a monthly meeting model (combined with the 90-Day Plan tool) ensures that leaders are consistently making progress toward their goals. This keeps their efforts from becoming a last-minute scramble. It also helps senior leadership recognize performance trends and quickly take action to knock down any barriers that might arise.

The Accountability Factor

As a leader, how do you hold people inside your practice (leaders and individual clinicians) accountable for meeting their goals? Let's say, for example, that you have a physician who is not capturing and charting the data elements necessary to support quality metrics. Therefore, she is losing revenue for the clinic by impacting your value-based payments.

These days a physician must do the right thing *and* correctly document having done the right thing if the practice is to get maximum reimbursement. The documentation step drives many physicians crazy—they simply don't see it as a necessary component of providing excellent clinical care. And yet, it is absolutely necessary in a value-based purchasing environment.

For example, a CMS "high-value" quality metric under MACRA is:
> *"The percentage of visits for patients aged 18 years and older during which the eligible professional attests to documenting a list of current medications using all immediate resources available on the date of the encounter. This list must include all known prescriptions, over-the-counters, herbals, and vitamin/mineral/ dietary (nutritional) supplements and must contain the medications' name, dosage, frequency, and route of administration."*

Taking the time to capture and document all of these, including dosage, frequency, and route of administration at every patient encounter, is a material change for how many clinicians were trained and have practiced for decades. And yet to be a high-performing value-based practice, this is something we must all learn to efficiently embrace.

Historically, not all clinicians were held accountable for minor transgressions like documentation shortfalls. In the past if a physician stepped out of line in some material way, his partners either ignored it or banded together to intervene as colleagues. Now that clinicians tend to be affiliated with larger health systems, and are subject to far more standards and expectations than existed in the past, there's a whole different dynamic.

In short, your practice needs a process for ensuring that clinicians and staff live up to your expectations and adhere to behavior standards. Just having a physician code of conduct hanging on the wall is not enough. Physician leaders need to actively hold themselves and other physicians to these standards.

Transparency and *reward and recognition* are incredibly powerful strategies. We regularly find that the most accountable organizations are also the most transparent. One reason is that when you know your colleagues' goals—

what's expected of them—you know how to support them. The other reason is plain old peer pressure. When people are watching, it's human nature to want to do your best work.

One of the highest performing organizations we know is OU Physicians, based in Oklahoma City. Clinicians not only share goals with each other but they share results. And this transparency isn't just between providers and staff—OU is actively working to share quality, patient experience, and other goals with their patients on the web.

Another example is John Peter Smith (JPS) Health, a public community healthcare system in Texas that posts its physicians' performance on the clinic reception area walls. Knowing that patients are reviewing their provider's and clinic's data while waiting to be seen has been a high motivator for leaders, clinicians, and staff. All team members are inspired to bring their A game. And as you would expect, they have seen a marked increase in the performance of the metrics they transparently share with their patients and community.

For eons, humans have known about the "stick and carrot" methods of getting people to comply. The stick is punishment. The carrot is reward. Transparency employs both techniques. If you're trying to improve diabetic patient care protocol, measure percent of doctors who are compliant with the protocol. Then you publicly recognize who is on top on a regular basis.

To be clear, we're not suggesting you publicly shame clinicians and staff who are falling short. The old adage about praising in public and criticizing in private certainly holds true here. The "stick" wielded in this case is the absence of the public recognition (along with personal financial impact of non-compliance of course).

By providing public recognition, leaders foster a high-performing culture. It's as simple as saying something like: "I want to manage up Tony this month. Tony has managed to increase his volume, improve his vaccination rates, and has also improved his patient experience results. Tony, would you share what you are doing with the rest of us?"

Changing behavior is a journey. Remember, many hospitals are further evolved in their thinking about performance management and accountability. Medical groups are just starting out. Give yourself grace as you work to close the gap if you are just starting out.

The journey begins with alignment and accountability, followed by incremental changes that move the practice toward high performance. The pace of these incremental changes should be based on the organization's ability to consistently practice them. Change too much too fast and you'll simply create new problems.

So the first and most important step is making sure you have the right management operating system in place. This is the foundation for everything, the track that your incremental change engine runs on. Then, stay focused on your strategic end goals as you slowly, surely, and relentlessly work toward them.

This way, every change you adopt will achieve highly sustainable results— and leaders, clinicians, and employees at every level will feel empowered and inspired to the next level of excellence...and the next...and the next.

CHAPTER 5

Creating a Patient-Centric Care Delivery Model

"One of the deep secrets of life is that all that is really worth
doing is what we do for others."
—Lewis Carroll

With the rise of consumerism and digitization in healthcare, the market
has fundamentally changed—just like virtually *all* markets. Think of it this
way: On the average smartphone with a reasonable number of apps, you can
order a pizza, reserve a hotel room, book a flight to Maui, and schedule a
vet appointment for your dog, all while listening to your favorite music and
reading an e-book. Why shouldn't you also be able to interact with your
physician?

You should of course. And thanks to existing technology—via telehealth or a
well-constructed patient portal—you can.

What we're trying to say is simple: With this level of consumer access to multiple types of healthcare services, the traditional model of building patient
care around physician availability is long gone. The focus today is on the
patient. This means that convenience and patient focus are (as they always
should have been) the right priorities when considering how to structure a
primary or specialty care model.

In part to respond to these market trends but also to address the high cost and other shortcomings of the U.S. healthcare system, the Institute for Healthcare Improvement developed a framework for improving healthcare called the "Triple Aim." This centers on three main goals:[1]

- Improving the patient experience of care (including quality and satisfaction)
- Improving the health of populations
- Reducing the per capita cost of healthcare

(For more about the Triple Aim, see Chapter 11.)

While initially aimed at the overall health system, this industry response easily translates to a way to organize and improve a medical group's models and systems of patient care. To place all this in context, a short history lesson is in order to highlight the fundamental change in the way care has moved to be more focused on patients across all the dimensions of service, treatment, and outcome.

Back in the late 1800s the A.T. Still University (then called the American School of Osteopathy) was thriving. Five trainloads of people a day poured into this remote area of Missouri to be treated by Dr. Andrew Taylor Still, the founder of osteopathy. Reportedly, trains were re-routed and boarding houses built to accommodate this influx of patients from all over the country.

Let's contrast these enthusiastic patients with their 21st century counterparts. Today in St. Louis, most people won't even cross the Missouri River to see a physician—no matter how good the physician might be. Sure, there are a few destination practices left (built around specialties like oncology), but overall the market has taken a 180-degree turn. Now, physicians are expected to meet patients where they are and when they want to be seen—whether that is in a retail clinic at a grocery store, an urgent care center, via a telehealth application, or in a traditional physician's office or clinic—not the other way around.

An academic study from the Mayo Clinic showed a causal relationship between the severity and acuity of a patient's health and his willingness to travel to see a physician. Not surprisingly, patients with less severe medical problems didn't travel far to see a physician while those with more severe diagnoses considerably increased the distance they were willing to travel.[2] When you consider that the majority of care provided is to patients with less severe medical problems, it's clear that we must pay attention to the results of this study.

As we discussed earlier, being patient-centric is no longer optional. Patient engagement is a critical differentiator for medical groups. This mostly means that patients are looking for individualized care tailored to their personal needs and timeframe, and care providers must figure out a way to give it to them. It used to be that medical group operations were built around the physician. Now it is the opposite. This means it's critical that you know who your patients are and what they want and expect from you.

Market forces have moved the consumer to the front and center of the value map. Call it the Amazon culture: Consumers want what they want, when they want it, and with all the information up front. Their preferences drive *everything*—and this is as true for medical groups as it is for booksellers, hoteliers, and banks.

This trend is impacting prices. Patients who rely on traditionally designed and operated medical practices are (understandably) becoming more and more frustrated that they can't get a straight answer to what should be a simple question: *How much is today's visit going to cost me?* Beyond co-pay, it's hard to say; the answer depends on what kind of insurance the patient has and how much of the deductible he's met.

This is why some retail medical practices are now saying: *Okay, regardless of what your insurance says, we're charging you $50.00 for an office visit.* Consumers are driving this change. Their feeling is, *Why would I come here if I don't know what I have to pay?* This is what it looks like when consumers exercise their market power.

All the dynamics are changing, and it's shaking up everything about the way we practice medicine. If a competitor wants to strike fear into your heart, they need only enter your market by building an urgent care center within a mile of your major hospital or medical practice site.

Markets Change Quickly—and Different Markets Have Different Needs

As cultural norms change, and as generations age, consumer demands evolve right along with them. Many people under 30 don't even have a physician. They use Teladoc, the "Uber" version of physician care, when they get sick. As they get older this tolerance for virtual visits changes. They'll want to see a specific physician in person—but if the consumer-centric culture holds, they'll still want instant access to that physician.

Retail clinics are an emerging force in healthcare. Patients can now go somewhere convenient, like a clinic staffed by nurse practitioners and located in a grocery or drug store, and later follow up with a specialist if needed. Urgent care clinics, too—with à la carte pricing like "$30 for a sports physical" and "$100 for an arm X-ray"—have sprung up at dizzying rates. These are the visible markers of a society in which the consumer rules—and the connected EHRs are the unseen ties that link them together and make them work.

The retail approach works quite well in Columbia, Missouri, where four universities are located. University of Missouri Health Care is a Huron client. When it started doing retail, it reported a 25 percent uptake in new patients. This young, healthy cohort has no problem being seen by a nurse practitioner. They've grown up in an on-demand culture. They appreciate being able to go in on a Sunday morning at 8:00 and be done by 8:15. In fact, they expect it.

However, the fact that a set-up works well in one area does not mean it will work well everywhere. We had one client in rural Oregon that (wrongly) assumed a retail strategy would work for them. People there don't mind going to urgent care—in fact, they like the quick access—so it seemed logical that they would accept retail. Yet as it turned out, patients absolutely *would not* go to retail clinics.

Here's why: Most people in that area are Medicare patients who are used to working with a physician. They view going to the doctor almost as a social event; they know the physicians because they are neighbors in a small community. If they started going to a retail clinic for regular appointments, they would have to see a nurse practitioner. They didn't mind seeing an NP for urgent care, but only because they knew their physician was right there in the same building and they could see her if they needed to.

Here's the lesson: It's important to *really* look at the patients you are serving and to understand what motivates them. This insight allows you to know what changes you need to make in order to meet their needs.

Next, we'll address some basic considerations that impact how the two types of practices—primary care and specialty—operate in our changing environment. Let's start with the practice the patient probably considers his "home base."

Primary Care Practices: Take a Chips & Bricks Approach

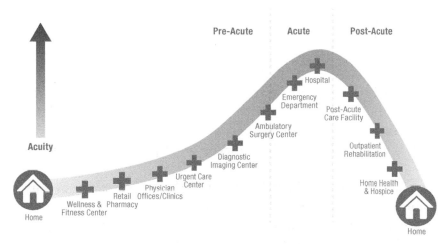

Figure 5.1 | The Continuum of Care Expressed as a Function of Acuity

As described above, most health systems well recognize the patient's preference for access and convenience. Moving to where the patient is requires multiple access points. That's why many organizations are putting their primary care practices out on the market in various ways—traditional physician offices, urgent care centers, fast tracks inside EDs, retail clinics, and telehealth systems. And they do this knowing that all of the above access points may need to attach to specialty practices as needed, via a patient-centered medical home (PCMH).

The PCMH model is designed to help primary care practices deliver more efficient care by creating more effective and predictable clinical outcomes over the course of a patient's interaction with the health system. It places an emphasis on having clinical and administrative staff working as a true team to manage patients over the long term, in order to care for them in a more standardized and streamlined way.

Medicare Part B has introduced legislation that singles out the PCMH model as a way to improve quality by proving that they're more effective. CMS is giving healthcare organizations enhanced reimbursement for placing patients in medical homes. To be classified as a medical home, the National Committee for Quality Assurance reports that you have to be favorably evaluated on the following key components:
  • Enhanced Access After Hours and Online
  • Long-Term Patient and Provider Relationships
  • Shared Decision Making
  • Patient Engagement in Health and Healthcare
  • Team-Based Care
  • Better Quality and Experience of Care
  • Lower Cost from Reduced Emergency Department and Hospital Use

There are many reasons for utilizing the PCMH model. Chief among these is to allow the primary care group to manage the continuum of care represented in Figure 5.1. Knowing why, where, and when a patient is receiving care is critical to success, especially in a value-based environment like the market is moving toward now.

What we're describing is Huron's Chips & Bricks^{SM} approach. The "bricks" are the physical (and in the case of telehealth, virtual) access points. The "chips" refers to the electronic health record that links the access points together.

The connected EHR is the centerpiece of the strategy. It's what allows a healthcare organization to see and understand the full spectrum of care a patient has received, no matter where he receives it.

The Chips & Bricks strategy allows medical groups to break patients down into consumer buckets: the soccer moms who need school physicals, the worried well, the over-65s, and so forth. They can also triage patients according to how sick they are and funnel them to the most appropriate locations. They can leverage advanced practice providers to care for the less sick and save their more specialized physicians for those patients with more complex and severe conditions.

By adopting a Chips & Bricks approach, you can build your practice in a strategic way that makes sense for specific types of patients—rather than being an undifferentiated "catch-all" doctor's office attempting to serve everyone who shows up. It's more efficient and cost-effective for the practice *and* it provides a smoother, faster experience for patients. Everyone wins.

A Few Thoughts on Getting Started

If you're deploying a Chips & Bricks strategy for primary care, a retail clinic might be a good starting point. Or you might set up your practice in a way that ensures most patients are seen at an urgent care. What's important is that patients have routine and regular contact with their primary care physicians at intervals to make sure the care continues to be appropriate.

Being innovative with practice structures may mean entering into arrangements with third parties such as drug stores or supermarkets. Before you start this process, it's critical to spend time assessing your organization's EHR capabilities and interfaces to ensure that you have the correct functionality. Also, be mindful of who you partner with. Make sure all parties have EHRs in place and are willing to allow patient information to flow freely across the system. If the answer is no, that's a big red flag. If you don't have access to the patient records across the entire continuum of care, it's not worth doing.

We must all be prepared to capture and track more data in meaningful ways so we can share it with payers, specialists, and others. Without end-to-end cross-system connectivity, it's impossible for primary physicians to stay engaged with their patients—and that engagement is crucial for ensuring positive clinical outcomes.

Once new locations are in place, be sure to communicate with patients *exactly* who your partners are. Don't assume they know. There might be several walk-in clinics in town, and there's a good chance your patients won't understand there's a difference unless you (aggressively and relentlessly) tell them. Of course you will have your logo on display there, but that's not enough.

Explain to patients—verbally, in marketing materials, in emails, in every way possible—that you are in a partnership with, say, the clinic in the Hy-Vee grocery store but NOT the one in Walmart. Assert to them that if they have a problem and your office is closed, they should go to the Hy-Vee. Why? Because the Hy-Vee clinic shares medical records with you, arranges referrals, fast tracks you to appointments, etc.—all of which allows for much better continuum of care.

In short, work hard to get the patient engaged with your practice and the overall health system it's affiliated with—not just with an individual clinician. The central message as you manage up your colleagues and the rest of the system should be that good continuum of care is the goal. By helping the patient improve and maintain better health—and by keeping her connected to the system that's familiar with her medical background—you're keeping her out of the ED and the hospital. This is what everyone wants.

Patient Engagement Starts at the Top

Over the years healthcare leaders have shifted their focus away from employee and physician *satisfaction* and toward employee and physician *engagement*. They've realized that there is a strong connection between engagement and crucial metrics like productivity and clinical quality. Now, they're starting to pay just as much attention to patient engagement—and for good reason.

As an industry we've realized that having patients actively involved in their own care is a great thing. Engaged patients take responsibility for their own health. They ask questions, give feedback, and comply with care instructions. And they're far more likely than disengaged patients to make the long-term lifestyle changes needed to prevent and control (expensive) chronic diseases.

In Chapter 9 we explain how patient engagement happens. It starts at the top of the organization with leaders, cascades to physicians and employees, and finally reaches patients. As you're building your patient-centric medical group or practice, we urge you to be mindful that engagement is a comprehensive strategy that impacts every person in your organization.

Now, before we move the discussion to specialty care practices, let's touch on care transitions. Despite the best intentions, patients don't get to stay exclusively in the primary care world forever. Conditions worsen, accidents happen, new problems strike, and they have to be admitted to the hospital, passed on to specialists, or both. What happens during these transitions can make all the difference in the continued well-being of patients—and in the economic health of the systems that care for them.

Transition of Care: Why It Matters So Much

As we've discussed throughout this book, our goal is to put the patient at the front and center so we can ensure that he gets better, stays well, uses fewer medical services, and once he leaves the hospital doesn't return. This requires close communication between healthcare organizations of all types. Transition of care—particularly when patients move out of the hospital and back into the hands of primary care and specialty care providers—matters more than ever.

Changes in federal reimbursement are a big part of the reason. For example, Medicare Part B and many other payers are moving rapidly into value-based reimbursement models that are reminiscent of managed care. A portion of reimbursement is tied to the quality of care the patient receives from surgery to recovery, for example, including physicians, skilled nursing facilities, home health agencies, and other providers. Another portion may be tied to specific care transitions such as reducing avoidable hospital readmissions. This is a "mega-trend" that is moving healthcare in a positive direction.

Obviously, these kinds of reimbursement arrangements force hospitals and medical practices to work together to make sure care is well coordinated, well executed, and cost effective. And one of the biggest concerns is making sure that patients don't have to return to the hospital too soon.

So if we know that poor communication is harming the long-term health of patients and costing hospitals money, why does it still happen? Part of it is due to the rise of hospitalists and intensivists. When hospital-based providers take over a patient's care, primary care providers simply don't do as much hospital rounding. It's easy for them to lose track of patients while they're hospitalized. This also raises the stakes on the quality of their EHR investment in that this is a major tool for addressing communication issues.

Also, rather than going home when they leave the hospital, many patients are moved to some sort of long-term acute care (LTAC) or intermediate care facility. When this happens, the physician who worked with the patient when he was hospitalized may not have privileges there. So she may hand over care to the LTAC or intermediate facility and not really know what happens to him after that.

The key for hospitals is to make absolutely sure that before a patient is discharged, follow-up appointments have been set with both his primary care physician and his specialist. One hospital we worked with did an internal study that found 75 percent of patients who did not have these two follow-up visits after discharge ended up being readmitted within two weeks.

Good, thorough communication is not just an issue at discharge. It needs to happen anytime a patient moves from the care of one clinician to the care of another. This includes handovers during the hospital stay. If you don't ensure there is continuity and good coordination of care, someone will end up reinventing the wheel and ordering a new battery of tests when it isn't needed—or the hospital stay will be extended unnecessarily.

Vic Arnold: The High Cost of Poor Transition of Care (A Personal Story)

A few years back, my wife, Dee Dee, had a severe infection that sent her to the emergency room of the local hospital. The situation turned quite serious as the physicians worked with her and she was sent to the ICU for 10 days. During the ICU stay, care coordination, handovers, and overall care were seamless. However, once she was moved to the general medicine floor, things fell apart a bit. The nursing staff, the hospitalists, and the attending physicians (surgeon and primary care physician) were not talking to each other, and as a result, orders got muddled, treatments were not coordinated, and Dee Dee ended up with a new problem, pneumonia, as a result of the lack of focus and care coordination.

Given the length of stay required to treat the first infection and now the pneumonia, the care coordinators became concerned about keeping Dee Dee in an acute care setting. This was a reasonable concern as she had gotten past the initial medical crisis and her pneumonia was well under control. The required care was shifting to be more routine in nature rather than the intensive level needed when she was admitted.

The hospital care coordinators proposed moving her to a brand new LTAC facility that had a good reputation. This made logical sense to Dee Dee and me, and initially we were fine with the decision. We felt it might even allow her to get home sooner. The nursing team began working on this move and soon things had progressed to the advanced planning stages.

The next day Dee Dee's surgeon and primary care physician both stopped by to round on her. We started talking to them about the planned move. Both looked at us quizzically and asked what this was about. It turned out they had not been informed of the planned move. To make matters worse, neither physician had admitting privileges to the LTAC. This meant they would not be able to follow her care there, nor would they have a direct way (other than through me) to know what was going on with her care.

On discovering this state of events, our family held a very intense discussion with the two physicians, the LTAC team, and the hospital nursing team. It was determined that Dee Dee would continue on at the hospital until she was ready to go home, and the LTAC facility would not be used for her care at all.

Chances are there was nothing wrong with the care she could have received at the LTAC. However, due to the lack of communication and the incomplete thought process associated with the handover, we no longer felt comfortable with this option. Dee Dee had received great care from the clinical team at the hospital and they likely saved her life from a very nasty infection. However, most of what we remember from the stay was the "dropped ball" on the failed plan to move her to the LTAC.

Specialty Care Practices: Fight the Forces That Block Patient-Centricity

The same issues we just discussed also apply when a patient is transitioning a) from a primary care provider to a specialist, and b) vice versa. Communication between physicians is crucial. There is nothing patient-centric about neglecting (or worse, refusing) to share vital information with another provider. And yet some specialty care providers are unwilling to hand over their patients' medical records.

We are *not* implying that most specialists are guilty of this. But because primary care providers are becoming more and more invested in the Chips & Bricks strategy we discussed earlier, they are more likely to be open with communication than their specialty counterparts. This reluctance to share information is one of the two big iron doors that stand in front of our efforts to create patient-centric specialty practices. (The other, which we'll discuss shortly, is difficulty in getting approval from insurance companies.)

Open Communication Is Everything

Our advice is simple: Insist that all healthcare providers inside your practice are open communicators. Hoarding medical records is "old school" thinking. It implies a mindset that you "own" the patient. (This is a vestige of the old "competition" paradigm and has no place in the new "collaboration" paradigm.) Or it may suggest that you simply don't want to take the time to link back to the primary care physician who referred the patient.

There is a movement underway to force healthcare organizations to give patients full access to their medical records and to provide referring physicians with those records as well. But even if medical record transparency wasn't a legal trend, it's the right thing to do—and the smart thing to do from a business perspective.

Being willing to share medical records is good referral management. When you treat primary care providers well, they will give you referrals. It begins with acknowledging that the primary care clinician is extending her reputation to you when she sends a patient to you. In return she expects you to (a) keep her in the loop, and (b) return the patient to her when you've done all you can for him. Doing both is a small price to pay to make sure you stay in the primary care provider's good graces.

It's vital for specialty practices to keep those referrals coming, especially now. In the days before value-based reimbursement, health systems saw referrals as revenue. If someone sent them a patient, that was a new infusion of money. Now, if someone refers a patient *away from* one of that system's employed specialists, it's an expense the system has pay to someone else. Do everything in your power not to let this happen.

Invest in Insurance-Savvy Staff Members

Now, let's talk about the second force that blocks patient-centricity inside specialty practices: insurance issues. Sometimes insurance companies won't approve a procedure the patient needs (or thinks he needs). Or maybe the procedure *would* have been approved if it were filed differently, but for some reason a staff member makes a mistake and the claim gets rejected. Obviously, incidents like these are big patient dissatisfiers.

Another serious problem is clinician and staff confusion around which care providers are in-network and which are not. Perhaps your practice is in a patient's network, but the lab or anesthesiologist you refer him to is not. Mistakes like this can happen easily—especially when a clinician is new to a community or when an insurance provider abruptly changes its policies. It's easy to imagine a patient's frustration and anger when he realizes after the fact that he has to pay hundreds of dollars out of pocket.

The best way to avoid insurance issues is to hire well. High-performing specialty groups know they must hire smart people and invest in healthy staffing ratios to stay on top of the rules of payment and to keep track of their referral network's payer contract statuses.

Insist on periodic meetings with the major payers in your market, whether they're government entities like Medicare and Medicaid or private insurance companies like Blue Cross Blue Shield and Aetna. Routine and regular communication with them on these sorts of topics may be painful but it's necessary to serve your patients' needs. It requires effort and manpower, and your practice cannot skimp on either.

Advanced Practice Providers Can Save You

Finally, let's swing back to an issue we touched on earlier in this chapter: leveraging advanced practice providers. As mentioned, primary care providers tend to be open to this strategy as it's a cornerstone of the Chips & Bricks approach. The same isn't always true for specialists. Many specialty physicians—especially those in the latter part of their career—have traditionally been resistant to the "team" approach.

We're pleased to say that this attitude is changing. For example, patients who go to a practice affiliated with Ronald Reagan UCLA Medical Center in Los Angeles for anything less than a compound fracture will see a physician assistant before they see an orthopedic surgeon. Those who go to Barbara Ann Karmanos Cancer Center in Detroit will see a nurse practitioner before they see an oncologist.

For the most part, patients are perfectly willing to see an APP as long as they don't feel they're being prevented from seeing the physician if they really need to. They appreciate being seen immediately and having their medical needs met quickly.

The benefits of this model to specialty practices are obvious. APPs can be practitioners in their own right. They can be wonderful resources for physicians who feel overwhelmed; they can handle a wide range of patient needs in a way that's safe, timely, and cost effective. In fact APPs can be instrumental in helping physicians achieve a healthier work-life balance and even avoid burnout.

Once physicians realize that using APPs doesn't detract from their ability to deliver excellent clinical outcomes and patient experiences, they will usually get on board. Here's an analogy we like: Michelangelo got the credit for painting the Sistine Chapel but the truth is he didn't do it alone. He had assistants who prepared surfaces and colors and surely completed many other tasks along the way. Like great artists of every stripe—and like every business leader who works with a team—no physician is an island.

Determining the Business You Are In

In the past, medical practice leaders didn't really think about marketing issues. Who you were going to see and how you were going to reach them were issues that were left up to chance. If anyone *was* thinking along these lines, it was probably the physician who founded the practice—certainly not anyone with a business strategy background.

All of that has changed. Now if you're a practice leader, or a system administrator who works with practice leaders, you have to pay attention. You have to be very focused, intentional, and strategic with your decisions. It's a matter of looking at your population and thinking about what makes sense.

Here are just a few of the factors you need to consider:

The predominance of large health systems in your area. In many major markets there has been massive consolidation. Often there are just two or three huge systems serving the entire patient population. If your practice is located in this type of market, you'll need to make your bets on who is going to be the leader and decide how you want to affiliate with that system.

Incidentally, employment or acquisition is not the only affiliation model. Joining a clinically integrated network is becoming an increasingly viable option.

Possible academic medical center (AMC) opportunities. Historically, most physicians who have been attracted to the AMC environment are not motivated solely by financial compensation. They enjoy teaching and research, and their commitment to their educational mission has superseded their desire to make a lot of money. But now, this idealism is butting up against deep funding cuts as well as the financial realities that are squeezing their for-profit counterparts.

Today, AMCs are now facing pressure to do much more clinical care than has been required in the past. This is making partnerships with outside medical practices seem far more feasible. At one time the litmus test was "faculty or not faculty." Now that line is blurring. When seeking affiliation opportunities, don't overlook your local AMC. They just might need your clinical expertise.

Payer mix. This factor has a huge impact on how you structure your practice. If 80 percent of your state's healthcare market is run by one insurance company (Blue Cross Blue Shield's presence in Alabama comes to mind), that's going to color how you think about the patients you are going to serve. Know the market you're in and make decisions accordingly.

Take the time to understand government payers, too: Medicaid, Medicare, VA, Tricare, Workers' Compensation, and so forth. This can certainly vary by geographic area. Medicaid in Oregon is a very different creature from Medicaid in Illinois or New York. Unusual as it may seem to East Coasters, Oregon office visit payment reimbursement is high compared to commercial payers.

Factor in all of these realities as you seek to balance your business and clinical needs. You might realize that you need to attract more of a certain kind of patient. If you're a group practice, should you open a primary care side in a different market? For mission-based reasons, a health system might purposely open clinics in underserved areas and become a federally qualified health center. At the same time, it might open a satellite office in a more affluent neighborhood to try to attract patients there.

Figure out what you can financially bear in terms of various mixes of payers. This includes factoring in which commercial payers pay well and which don't. At the time of this writing, we have one client who is trying to decide whether to keep taking fee-for-service business at all or whether to move to managed care patients only.

All of these decisions need to be revisited monthly or at least quarterly. This may seem frequent, but practices that stay in business know they have to be that vigilant.

Demographics. Patient preferences for care providers of specific genders and cultural naturally evolve over time as attitudes change and populations shift. For instance, it used to be that OB/GYN was a male-dominated specialty; now it's turned around and is almost exclusively a woman's domain.

Diversity is a great thing and a goal to strive for. Smart practices strive to keep a thoughtful balance between making sure the medical staff mirrors the racial/cultural/gender makeup of their community and keeping an eye on expertise and clinical capability.

Chances are, the demographic makeup of your care providers will naturally shift along with your patient base. But if you happen to have a practice whose physicians look completely different from your patient base, start taking steps to remedy the divide—don't just wait for it to happen. This is what it means to respond to consumer forces.

Matching specialties to patient need. Specialty follows pathology. Look at the diseases that affect high numbers of people in your area. If your health system is in a state with high numbers of smokers, like Kentucky, New York, and Louisiana, you may want to more prominently feature pulmonary and oncology services. If you're in Colorado, with its higher altitude and greater sunlight, you might need more dermatology oncologists and MS specialists. If you're in California, Florida, or Arizona, where there are a higher number of retirees, you'd want a higher mix of infectious disease and rheumatology.

These are only a few of the factors that go into a patient-centric practice design. However, they will get you started thinking in the right direction. Now that you have read this chapter, we'd like you to consider your own practice or group in light of what you've learned. Here is a quick assessment:

How "Patient Centered" Is Your Practice?

Here is a checklist to help you decide. Can you answer "yes" to most of these statements?

- When making decisions about operations and overall practice management, the question "Is it good for the patient?" is always asked and answered with a *yes*.
- Access to care is provided in as many locations and "venues" as reasonably possible—traditional physician's office/clinic, retail, telehealth, urgent care, etc.
- Practice work hours support "off-hour" appointments—specifically, after 5:00 p.m. Monday through Friday and also on weekends.
- Each member of the care team, from medical assistant to medical doctor, is allowed and encouraged to practice to the top of their license and support the expanded access requirements that support patient-centered care.

- Online access to information—both educational regarding specific clinical needs and actionable in terms of making appointments or receiving test results—is available to patients. Your system supports both traditional e-health (laptop, etc.) and m-health (a.k.a. smartphone) formats with appropriate security to ensure information is shared *only* with the right people.
- Communication with specialists and health systems is timely, accurate, and robust.
- Care transition for referrals and discharge planning from acute care and outpatient setting and related areas are well coordinated. Neither the patient nor the patient's family are required to be the main coordination points for this care.
- Patient personal needs like reasonable transportation, directions, expectation setting, and related basic communication are as simple, easy, and direct as possible.
- Telephone systems are efficient, patient friendly, and easy to navigate; phone trees are simple; calls are answered by a person; and, when needed, transferred calls are completed with an agent on the line.

In conclusion, our industry is almost unrecognizable compared to how it used to look. We once practiced medicine "responsively," based largely on who happened to come in the door. Now it's a new day, and to survive we have to get very strategic and intentional. That means everything about your practice will be personalized and quite different from other practices, driven by the realities of the market you're trying to serve.

How you govern your medical group and what you focus on as you govern will determine how successful you are. In the next chapter, we will cover some issues related to this subject.

CHAPTER 6

Governance and Leadership Structures: Setting Up a Practice That Works

"Courage is what it takes to stand up and speak. Courage is also what it takes to sit down and listen."
—Sir Winston Churchill

"Governance: the way that a city, company, etc. is controlled by the people who run it."
—Merriam-Webster.com

This chapter is about medical group governance. It's appropriate to start out by asking: *What* is *governance anyway*? If it's a dictionary definition you want, refer to the Merriam-Webster one above. But if you're looking for a way to think about what lies at the heart and soul of the task, we prefer the Churchill quote directly above that—the one about courage.

It's true. Governing large groups of clinicians—often numbering in the hundreds or even thousands—and all the other healthcare professionals who support their work is no task for the faint of heart. It requires a group of smart, tough, thoughtful people who are willing to listen, to take a stand, and to make the hard decisions that go into empowering medical practices to fulfill their life-saving missions to the best of their abilities.

Too often, medical groups and the health systems that they are connected to don't approach the subject with the seriousness it deserves. That needs to change. Great clinicians and other healthcare professionals want to work for well-run organizations. If you want them to join you, and more to the point stay with you, make sure you're giving them a practice where they can do their best work.

Previously when people said "physician governance," they were referring to clinical behavior management. But now that 66 percent of physicians are employed by a health system in some form or fashion, the phrase has taken on new meaning.[1] As medical practices have gotten bigger and more complex, so has the task of keeping them running smoothly and efficiently.

In our work at Huron with medical groups, we see the importance of governance firsthand. We find that organizationally ineffective governance models, combined with inept or under-built management teams, are easily the number one reason medical practices struggle to meet the patient needs of their market and fail to meet their health system's expectations.

The specific model of governance can be a bit variable. Practices need as much management as they can stand. Keep in mind "form follows function to governance." You want to create a system that provides informational and accountability awareness without becoming a bureaucracy. That means putting in place just enough internal controls to allow the practice to make decisions quickly and crisply and to ensure that there is no confusion about who is responsible for what.

Take note: When rank-and-file physicians are saying, "I don't know who to go to with my problem so I just talk to a board member," you know you have an organization with a governance problem. We find that many medical groups have the problem from time to time—and it's not hard to understand why.

Governance and Management Infrastructure Have Not Kept Up with Size

The root of the problem is that most practices have been very slowly built over time. Their infrastructure has evolved incrementally from a starting point that once made sense—with a practice manager running the administrative show and working for the physician owners/partners—*without* thoughtful restructuring to create the kind of governance and management platform needed to meet today's needs.

Organizations tend to make incremental changes in response to problems rather than taking the time to deliberately put in place the right management structure, leadership team, and clear performance expectations that match the span of control needed given their size, geographic market, relationships to larger health systems, etc. This is a common problem and a tough pattern to break. However, we *must* break it if we're to meet the far more complex leadership needs of today's medical groups and physician organizations.

Here's an example. At Huron we worked with a prosperous Texas health system that uses hospital-based physicians. When we started to work with them, we discovered that while there was a robust medical group with a strong leadership team, the hospital CEO had the Emergency Department leader reporting directly to him and the physician leader personally in charge of scheduling all 200 ED physicians.

This created a couple of big problems. First, the physician leader had no time to do anything else. He couldn't really be a leader at all. Second, because of the reporting relationship, the ED physician leader and his team were not really working together with the other members of the medical group to support the health system's clinical or administrative goals and objectives. While there were good leaders all around, they did not have a cohesive governance model. These circumstances marginalized the effectiveness of ED operations, the medical group, and the health system.

Our solution was direct and simple. The ED physician leader was moved to report directly to the medical group's physician dyad. This meant the ED physician leader reported to the physician CEO, and the administrative leader was moved to report to the COO. The medical group added the needed infrastructure to support the ED leader and to support the hospital CEO's need for an effective management model. Finally (and most importantly), we enabled the ED physicians to have regular, structured, direct interaction with their peers in patient care by setting up a clinical management process that included the hospitalists, intensivists, and other specialists. This allowed them to more effectively address the care coordination and patient transition needs of the health system. It turned out to be a "win" for all involved.

As we've said throughout this book, practices *must* get more purposeful about how they manage themselves. Making this change will require much more expertise at the governance and leadership levels than we've had in the past. Governance is especially crucial as a practice grows. Once there are between 50 and 100 physicians in a practice, there *must* be an effective management structure in place.

This size is hardly unusual. We at Huron and Studer Group® regularly work with organizations that have thousands of affiliated clinicians. With all the consolidations and acquisitions occurring across the healthcare industry, very large practice groups are becoming the norm. It's time smart practice governance caught up with the trend.

Command and Control Doesn't Work with Physicians

Once a hospital system acquires or otherwise joins forces with a medical group (which may itself have expanded drastically over the course of just a few years), administration leaders quickly realize that a new governance structure needs to be put in place. The problem comes when they fail to realize that what works for hospitals simply won't work for medical practices.

Hospital systems have a sharply defined "command and control" structure in terms of management functions: CEO, CNO, CMO, CIO, COO, etc. This hierarchical system cascades down to vice presidents, directors, and so forth. Yet medical groups typically are *not* top-down organizations. They tend to have fewer layers. This is the fundamental difference between medical groups and other providers like hospitals. As Robert Wachter described in his book *The Digital Doctor: Hope, Hype, and Harm at the Dawn of Medicine's Computer Age*:

> *"One of the great challenges in healthcare is that medicine is at once an enormous business and an exquisitely human endeavor; it requires the ruthless efficiency of the modern manufacturing*

plant and the gentle hand-holding of the parish priest; it is about art; it is imminently quantifiable and yet stubbornly not."[2]

Therefore, the leadership and governance model of a medical group needs to be built to address these differences. Specifically, physician organizations call for more of a management structure where leadership is shared across the organization to address both clinical and administrative functions where the "workers" (the physicians) cross these boundaries routinely in ways very unlike and not well suited to traditional command and control leadership and governance models. Failing to understand and take into account the different nature of management and governance in a medical group is a frequent source of trouble and organization dysfunction.

Here is an example. A large southern medical group we worked with made the mistake of taking a "command and control" approach with performance improvement initiatives. The health system CEO set a goal for infection rates; he picked a number out of the air and stated, "We want to reduce infection rates by 40 percent." Then, leaders jammed it down through the organization rather than allowing physicians the autonomy to say, "Let's work out what reducing infection rates means in the context of my own individual practice. And then, considering your 'ideal world' goal, let's try to meet in the middle."

When you realize that hospitals and medical groups are fundamentally different animals, you can govern in a way that respects both—and doesn't let the needs of one party overwhelm the needs of the other.

Structure of a Typical Medical Group

As we mentioned earlier, around 66 percent of physicians are now in some sort of an employment or affiliation arrangement. That means it's now typical for a medical group to have a relationship to a parent health system. The medical group is its own organization but it's also subsidiary to the health system—much in the same way that Dasani is a subsidiary of Coca-Cola.

Because it's often easier to show than to tell, we've included the following graphic to depict the relationship. This illustration depicts a traditional medical group leadership dyad model for large health systems that's built around each service line (such as cardiovascular care) and includes all delivery models (inpatient, ambulatory, telemedicine).

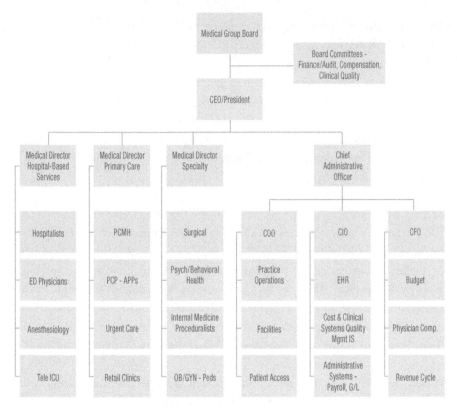

Figure 6.1 | Traditional Medical Group Structure

It is critical to note that several of the larger clinic organizations in the country are now embarking on a transformation past the common clinic structure shown above and are integrating acute care and outpatient surgical center and other similar services into their operations. Due to this, they are moving to an expanded service line model whereby the financial and administrative accountability is placed on the vertical axes of these organizations while the clinical and population health-oriented accountability is placed on the horizontal axes.

The service lines reside on the horizontal axes and organize around specific patient/disease types (orthopedics, oncology, cardiology, etc.) in order to unify the approach to care for the patient across the organization. On the vertical axes reside the administrative and clinical employees and their reporting structure as well as shared functions like patient access, urgent care, retail sites, ambulatory surgery centers, ancillaries, acute care, and other operations that support direct patient care service lines. The administrative functions are organized around a shared service model to allow appropriate cross health system operations efficiency.

Leaders of all of these operations report within a dyad model to a CEO who is sometimes a senior physician leader who, in turn, reports to a unified board that is responsible for the mission, vision, and values of the overall organization.

Medical Group Leadership Roles

Let's take a quick look at the critical leadership roles inside a medical practice group.

President or Chief Executive Officer (CEO). In the past this role was often filled by a physician with a few decades of practice behind him; he was burned out and ready to move on to something new. This is no longer a reasonable choice given the demands now required of this position. It has become a critical job with very strong, specific requirements. While physicians with strong leadership and management backgrounds have increasingly taken this role, it is not a prerequisite. One key leading practice that addresses the need for management expertise is to team this role directly with a strong chief administrative officer or chief operating officer.

The medical group president/CEO must be able to work collaboratively and must have strong leadership skills that promote a team approach within the organization. She has fiduciary responsibility for the medical group.

This leader often reports to the CEO of the larger health system and is part of the health system's executive team. There should be no barrier between them.

If so, it's a red flag that the leadership of the health system doesn't perceive the value of the partnership.

It's vitally important that the president/CEO is able to truly partner with the health system. If she hasn't worked in that setting herself, she must at least be able to understand the basic operations and day-to-day challenges of running a hospital and health system.

What Does a Great Medical Group President Look Like?

Here is a checklist of important traits for this leader:

1. If the CEO is a physician, then she must be a practicing physician at least 20 percent of the time if the group is really large, meaning 500 or more clinicians. If the group is smaller, then she should practice 30 percent of the time. This allows her to maintain an understanding of the "pulse" of the medical group. And it almost goes without saying that she needs to be a solid performing clinician whose example is one other doctors can aspire to.

2. Grounded in a general understanding of the clinical and medical-economic facts of the region the medical group serves. Also, she is currently active in the local business and social community (or at least is willing to become).

3. Strategic thinker who is able to move strategy into action.

4. Transparent and honest. She must maintain the confidence of the medical group board.

5. Completely devoted to the medical group. There must be no conflicts of interest or commitment (including no *appearance* of such conflicts).

6. History of working collaboratively and well with a group of individuals.

7. Willing to listen to input and able to admit when she is wrong— and resolve problems that arise because of it.

8. Able to balance a strong sense of business and what is right for the patients served by the medical group.

9. Comfortable with delegating tasks and working with a strong administrative leader in a dyad to drive the clinical and business aspects of the medical group.

10. Well-versed in the knowledge of payer contracts and contracting along with specialty-specific reimbursement trends. She is comfortable with value-based reimbursement contracts and models.

Chief Administrative Officer (CAO) or Chief Operating Officer (COO). There are a variety of titles for this position, depending on the organization. In academic medical centers, people who fill this role are often called executive directors or associate deans of clinical affairs. CAOs/COOs execute the strategy of the medical group as determined by the board and directed by the president/CEO. They do so by managing the clinical operations of Ancillary Services, Front Desk Operations, Practice Management Functions, Information Technology, Finance, and HR. They often have marketing and business development responsibilities that are shared with the president/CEO. They must be able to collaborate and function with the appropriate shared service or other operating components of a health system in those cases where there is an affiliation or more direct relationship with a parent organization.

A person who fills this role often has advanced healthcare business and leadership training (i.e., MBA, MHA, MPH, MPA, CPA, or the equivalent). He needs 10-plus years of practical experience as a baseline. What's more, he needs to know the healthcare business inside and out. He needs a fundamental understanding of finance and operations. He needs an understanding of insurance payer contracts and even business law, since healthcare is such a highly regulated industry.

If you are taking on a CAO/COO role, it helps if you've crossed back and forth a bit between working in a hospital setting and in a medical practice setting (almost in an apprenticeship fashion). It's not that you must have started at the very bottom of an organization but you do need to have had a series of progressively responsible jobs. We've found that quite often the most

well-rounded senior executives are those who have both finance and people
(HR) experience.

Vic Arnold: My Time on the Front Lines of Medical Records

At a critical point in my career, I was a senior leader at a prestigious
academic medical center. I worked in IT. We were very progressive,
and electronic health records were a relatively new concept at the
time. We felt that digitizing medical information was the way to go
and pressed system leadership to fund a large project. Before funding
was approved, the wise system COO required me to spend 30 days
working as a manager in the medical records department.

The experience was a revelation. There were endless details to manage. Individual data points seemed to come from everywhere at any
time, and all of it was supremely confidential. It was manageable but
daunting to realize up close that if even one detail got lost it could be
potentially life threatening to a patient. I knew this in the abstract,
but my time in medical records made it very real and personal.

Though I had over 10 years of experience in healthcare at the time, it
couldn't have prepared me for this. I had to learn a whole new aspect
of healthcare in a very big hurry. We got the funding, but only after
gaining a better understanding of medical records management. It
was not easy but was worth it for the perspective I gained. There is
no substitute for hands-on experience in the trenches.

There is a trend toward bringing in someone from another industry and putting him in a senior-level position. This rarely works well, no matter how
brilliant a leader the person was in a previous industry. Healthcare is very
complex and there is just so much value in having decades of industry experience behind you. (It's okay if you come from another industry, but you should
gain some healthcare experience before ascending to the highest levels.)

The CAO/COO should have a **director of practice operations** reporting to him. He needs to think carefully about how he provides a leadership structure for the medical group at the operating level. He must truly understand the market he is serving—to be able to operationally support the practice so it has the fewest barriers to access. It is up to him to make it possible for the practice to differentiate itself in the market.

The director of practice operations must work closely with the **medical directors** of the various service lines that the medical group needs to link clinical effectiveness with operations efficiency. The medical director role is an important one in both large and small medical groups. These individuals (who generally report to the CEO) must have deep clinical experience in their respective fields of medical practice but must also have the ability to work collaboratively on matters of quality and patient and physician engagement. They must also understand and appropriately advocate for resources from the operations team all while serving the needs of patients and colleagues via direct care and sometimes direct supervision.

Acquisitions Leader: A Critical Role for Growing Organizations

If your health system or medical group is in acquisition mode, you should have an operating leader who reports to the CAO/COO and is responsible for acquisitions. (In fact, it may be two people if more bandwidth is needed.)

To be clear, this is not a business development role. In fact, while there does need to be a strong handover from whoever manages the acquisition process in its early stages, the role described here is separate. This person—let's call her "acquisition leader"—helps acclimate the group to the larger health system or medical group after the terms and conditions of sale or affiliation are complete.

After a couple of years have passed, this leader moves on to the next group that has been acquired. She has to have good "soft skills" to be able to help people make the transition. She must also be able to see the "good" and "bad" in both the old ways and new ways of doing things so that the right compromises can be made and problems can be resolved during the acquisition process.

Finally, the CAO/COO must work well together with the CEO of the medical group. This has to be a close relationship of trust. Similarly, he must have a strong relationship with the COO of the larger health system. As you can see, this is a pivotal role. We can't say enough about how important it is to get the right person in place.

Chief Financial Officer (CFO). In addition to having a CAO/COO, once a medical group crosses the line of approximately 100 physician members, it should appoint someone to organize and manage the finances of the medical group. This person's title is often chief financial officer (CFO). For the larger organization, this is a critical role, and the profile of this individual is similar to that of other CFOs with the understanding that size determines scope and function. Whoever fills the CFO function should have specific experience with provider compensation, physician revenue cycle concepts, and related medical group issues. This role is part of the leadership "triumvirate" that helps the medical group manage operations and finances successfully on a day-to-day basis and in conjunction with strategic initiatives undertaken by the board.

Operating Board. If your medical group is an independent organization or operates in a state with corporate practice of medicine laws, it is advisable to have a working board of directors to assist the leadership team with fiduciary and strategic management. Even more important, this board defines, sustains, and sometimes redefines the mission of the medical group.

Keep in mind: Though many practices seem not to realize this, a high-performing board is critical. In fact, we believe it is a "make or break" factor. Ineffective boards make for unhealthy medical groups. If you don't have an effective board, you'll notice high turnover in the senior roles (CEO and CAO/COO).

The major responsibilities of the board are generally the following:
- Strategic planning and implementation
- Hire the president/CEO of the medical group
- Oversight of hiring, evaluation, and compensation of the administrative and clinical staff
- Formulation and oversight of major by-laws and policies of the board and the practice
- Review and adopt the annual budget
- Review financial and clinical performance on an advisory basis

For those physician organizations that are now part of larger health systems, the need for a fiduciary board is not necessary as that is addressed by the health system. In this case, we like to see that one or more of the physician organization physician leaders are members of the health system board. They still have the responsibilities listed above as members of this larger health system board, and it is important that the right physician leader(s) be appointed.

Replacing the board at the level of the physician organization is often some form of regional or other operating unit council. This council has responsibility for the well-being of the physician organization and ensures that the organization is aligned with the large health system's goals and objectives.

A Few Final Thoughts on Boards and Other Models

We'd be remiss if we closed this chapter without addressing what to do when a board or a health system council just isn't working. Sometimes they become dysfunctional or ineffective and you may need to change the membership. Thankfully this rarely happens. It may be appropriate to bring in someone from the outside who has experience with this situation to advise you on the best steps to take to resolve it.

Education is the starting point for addressing organization dysfunction. You may need a "senior statesman" type to come in and meet with individual board members and educate them on what their role should be. Once they have clarity around this, and everyone is on the same page, they can decide whether they want to remain on the board or not.

If you'll recall, in earlier chapters we touched on Studer Group's Evidence-Based Leadership[SM] framework (which allows organizations to align goals, actions and processes, and execute quickly) and its Leadership Evaluation Manager® tool (which helps leaders understand the key items they are accountable to achieve and which of those should take the highest priority). Both of these foundation builders are invaluable for helping board and council members stay aligned with the direction and goals of the organization. To learn more about these tools in addition to other tactics Huron and Studer Group offer, visit www.studergroup.com/medical-group.

Don't underestimate the importance of creating and sustaining a solid governing framework. There can be no doubt that the success of your medical group or practice depends on getting this right. Take your time, do your due diligence, and get the best people in place. Your physicians, employees, and ultimately your patients will thank you for putting in the work upfront.

CHAPTER 7

Designing Your Brand Experience

"Authentic brands don't emerge from marketing cubicles or advertising agencies. They emanate from everything the company does…"
　—Howard Schultz, CEO & Chairman of Starbucks

"Your brand is what other people say about you when you're not in the room."
　—Jeff Bezos, CEO & Chairman of Amazon

We've touched on the crucial importance of getting clear on your mission, vision, and values and allowing that to shape how you market yourself. We've talked about the specific populations you want to serve. And we've covered some leadership practices and systems you need to hardwire into your practice in order to serve your chosen patients to the best of your ability.

Now it's time to start thinking about what patient-centricity looks like for *your* practice. Depending on who your patients are—Men? Women? Children? Teens? Seniors?—serving them well can have many different meanings.

In all cases you want to deliver excellent care. That's a given. But how you go about delivering that care can vary wildly. Consider the difference between getting your morning coffee at McDonald's versus getting it at Starbucks.

Both transactions produce a piping hot cup of coffee, right? But they also produce very different brand experiences (and at vastly different price points).

Visiting a medical practice is no different. When you look at the goods and/or services you're providing in exchange for payment, it seems pretty simple. The patient is getting a strep test or an X-ray or having a prescription refilled. But what kind of experience do you want your patients to have while they're getting this done?

The answer is: It depends on who your patients are. It's not possible to be "generically" patient-centric. Patients are people and people are incredibly diverse. You need to be patient-centric *in the context of* the populations you are serving.

For example, if you're catering to men, what *kind of* men? Are they Wall Street bankers? Or are they rural blue collar workers? The answer should impact everything from your décor to the magazines you place in the reception area. (Sure, there are always exceptions, but for the most part, people who read *The Economist* are very different from those who read *Field & Stream*.)

And of course "patient-friendly" isn't even where your efforts should end. Your practice should also be *family*-friendly. In other words, do your exam rooms easily accommodate family members who might be tagging along? Is the restroom near the waiting area or is it a long hike away with lots of confusing twists and turns? Are patients likely to bring children with them, and if so, does your waiting area make them feel welcome?

We once visited an OB practice that was designed to look and feel like a spa. Furnishings were plush and luxurious. Soothing aromas filled the air. Fresh cut flowers and bubbling tabletop fountains added to the serene ambience. It was beautiful—yet for some reason practice leaders were finding that patients weren't coming back to have their second or third child.

We quickly realized why. There was nothing to accommodate the small children who, inevitably, come to the doctor's appointment with many expectant moms. If this practice had been on the Upper East Side of Manhattan, where many patients have nannies, it would have been perfect. But in this location (and the vast majority of the U.S.) there should have at least been a corner stocked with blocks and coloring books. (And there certainly should *not* have been breakable vases within arm's length of curious little hands.)

To Unify or *Not* to Unify? That Is the Branding Question

Deciding to make a particular location look and feel a certain way is only a small part of your task. Many of the people reading this book don't just have a single location to brand. Chances are you work for a medical group with multiple locations. If this is true for you, then you need to decide: Will all of the practices have a unified brand? Or will each be branded separately?

This is a critical question and there's no right or wrong answer. But if you do decide to create a unified brand, then you have to create a common brand *experience*. Too many practices fail to understand this. Brand is not just about the name and logo on the door—it's about the brand promise that comes with the name and logo.

Medical Groups Are Your Health System's Front Door

If you want to build your brand, reputation, and market share, then you must focus on your health system's physician offices. Eighty-five percent or more of your community will visit a physician in your market this year while less than 7 percent will spend a night in a hospital.[1]

According to data from the U.S. National Center for Health Statistics, for every U.S. inpatient stay, there are:[2,3,4]
- 3.5 hospital outpatient visits
- 3.7 ED visits
- 26.2 medical practice visits

One academic medical center (AMC) we worked with decided that, practically speaking, each specialty could make its own decisions and go its own way. Each would determine its own electronic health records, create its own patient registration process, set its own scheduling processes, do its own billing, and so forth. Yet despite every specialty doing its own thing, the AMC put its logo on every door in an attempt to brand it all as one big system.

This is a classic mistake. If you do brand yourself as a system, patients expect you to *act* as a system. If a patient has to start over with giving you their information every time they visit another practice inside the system (or an affiliated facility)—or has to deal with different billing departments—it's frustrating and anxiety producing. It certainly doesn't create loyalty to the brand. In fact, it breaks the brand promise.

That's exactly what was happening with the AMC we just described. They found that patients in the sports medicine practice, for instance, weren't naturally transitioning over to the orthopedic practices affiliated with the system. Patients were discovering that, despite the presence of the AMC's logo, every practice did its own thing. As a result, they would become loyal only to the individual practice—not the overarching brand. In fact, in this case, the overarching AMC brand experience was creating so much chaos and confusion that they actually were losing patients from both the health system and the specialty practices to a new unified-branded health system in town.

To be clear, there's nothing wrong with deciding to create a unified brand. There's also nothing wrong with *not* doing so. Plenty of big health systems acquire medical practices and purposely don't rebrand them. When patients visit their doctor's office, they often don't even realize he or she is affiliated with a big national system.

Regardless of which choice you make, be aware that there are pros and cons associated with each.

One advantage of creating a unified brand is *identity*. Patients associate the different pieces as parts of the whole. They start to connect the dots on how the care continuum works. This makes it easier to convince them to stay within your provider network—and since you've hopefully unified all your systems and processes to support your unified brand, it's easier to keep serving them across services and locations.

On the other hand, the big disadvantage is this: If one part of your system fails to live up to the brand experience you're working so hard to create, it pulls the whole brand down. Imagine how you'd feel if you walked into a Starbucks franchise and had a dismal experience: The coffee was cold, the barista was rude, the floor was filthy. Chances are it would taint your view of Starbucks as a whole, wouldn't it? The same is true of a commonly branded medical group.

What we're discussing here is an important strategic decision. Don't let marketing make the decision alone. And be careful about rushing into a unified brand if you haven't laid the underpinning to deliver a unified patient (brand) experience. You'll only create a lot of frustration and anxiety for patients and it will be worse than if you hadn't pretended to be unified in the first place.

To return to the Starbucks analogy, imagine a scenario where you take your Starbucks loyalty card into a store and the barista says, "We don't have you in our system. To use your loyalty card here, I'm going to need you to redo your registration form. Will you fill out this form?" Now imagine every time you go into a new Starbucks this happens again. Pretty soon the value of that loyalty card will become non-existent. In fact it will become more annoying than beneficial.

Fifteen "Commonalities" a Unified Brand Must Have

1. A single contact point to schedule appointments
2. ...to resolve billing questions
3. ...to get prescriptions refilled
4. The way you answer the phone (New clinic name? Old clinic name? A "bridge" option like *This is XYZ Clinic, a part of Good Medicine Health System?*)
5. The way you greet people when they walk in your office
6. A common check-in process
7. A single time in the process when co-pays are collected (and the ability to always know how much the cost will be ahead of time)
8. A common new patient form

9. A shared EHR so patients won't have to provide medical history ten times
10. Consistency in clinical interaction
11. A single way to manage waits and delays (for instance, all locations send a text to let patient know the clinician is running behind)
12. A standardized checkout process, including how referrals are handled
13. A common patient portal providing e-services common across locations and specialties
14. A standardized service recovery process
15. Consistency in key words and phrases used by all members of the team (AIDET® is a good example)

If, after reading this section and the rest of the chapter, you *do* decide to create a unified brand experience, we urge you to "lean in" and do it right. Decide what it should look and feel like. Make hardwiring it a very deliberate effort. Be sure you and everyone affiliated with your system understand the *why* behind it. Invest in the training to make sure everyone has the skills to live it. Finally, make sure that—to paraphrase a quote we like—the mission, vision, and values that define your brand don't just hang on the walls but walk in the halls.

Regardless of your decision, there are elements that are critically important to creating a patient-centric brand experience. Let's discuss some of the most important ones next.

Creating the Right Clinic Environment

Much of a patient's experience is connected to the physical location where he actually receives care. When he "goes to the doctor," he actually visits a place—a building with a parking lot, walls, and ceiling—where certain interactions happen. So many nuances go into making this physical location truly patient-centric. Many of them are overlooked by leaders (or at least given only cursory attention), yet together they have great impact on how patients perceive their care.

Location, Location, Location

Too often leaders pick locations based on what *they* like or on meaningless factors like prestige. They don't think, *Given the clientele we're serving, is this an appropriate location?* They don't always consider practical issues like parking, access to public transportation, access to other relevant services, safety of the neighborhood, and so forth. Yet all of these matter when targeting a demographic.

For example, if you're catering to lower socioeconomic patients, you'll need to make sure your practice is accessible based on mass transit in the area. Are your hours synced with bus or train schedules? If the train stops at the station by your office at 7:50 and you don't open until 8:00, you'll be leaving a bunch of people standing outside in the cold for 10 minutes. This may seem like a little thing, and many practice leaders don't think about it at all when they set their office hours, but those 10 minutes really matter to patients when it's 10 degrees outside and the wind is blowing.

If you have a lot of patients who are seniors, you'll need to think about accessibility. How many handicapped parking spots do you have? How ADA accessible are you? It's one thing to simply meet ADA compliance, but if a patient has to walk halfway around the building to get to the special door with the elevator, "compliance" won't seem very impressive. Far better to choose a location with direct entry that's accommodating to physically challenged patients.

We visited a gerontologist's office that had three crumbling cement steps leading up to the front door. Even the most sure-footed 80-year-old patient probably isn't going to appreciate climbing those steps to get to this care provider. This building also wouldn't be a good choice for a pediatric practice (whose patients are pushing baby strollers) or an orthopedic practice (whose patients must navigate with crutches and wheelchairs).

Here's a good example: We met with an audiologist who told us, "I chose this office because it's great for people who have hearing *and* sight issues." She went on to explain, "When you lose your vision, your hearing becomes incredibly important, so I happen to have a lot of blind and sight-impaired people as patients. I wanted a location that would be a good fit for them."

The audiologist purposely chose a location close to mass transit with this patient population in mind. She also made sure the building had elevators instead of stairs since they're so much better for people who must maneuver with canes. She made sure they installed Braille signage in the hallways. Finally, when last we spoke, she was looking to bring in an ophthalmologist to practice next door so that people can get both hearing and eye care together.

When you really think through what your patients' lives are like and make decisions accordingly, you can lay the groundwork for an incredible patient experience. There's a child-oriented family practice in Colorado that really illustrates the point. This practice opened inside a strip mall that also houses a Toys "R" Us. The practice leaders partnered with Toys "R" Us to provide discounts to patients.

Think about that. Parents can take their kids to the doctor and then go to the toy store afterward with a coupon the clinic provided. Oh, and in the same shopping complex there's a Red Robin restaurant. So after going to the doctor, then the toy store, parents can take the kids to eat at a family-friendly restaurant. This practice is really helping customers take what could be a scary or unpleasant experience for their kids and turn it into a fun family event.

It's brilliant strategy—and it really *is* a strategy. Just down the road from this strip mall location is a new, more prestigious building that contains other medical practices. The practice could have chosen it but chose the mall—on purpose—for the reasons we've just described.

Décor/Ambiance

Similarly, practice owners need to pay close attention to how their practices are decorated, what kind of music is playing, and what kind of entertainment items they provide for patients. Do your choices *truly* fit patient needs?

Think back to the OB practice we discussed earlier in the chapter. The elegant surroundings that no doubt appealed to their patients' "serene spa enthusiast" side turned out not to work so well for their "demanding toddler-wrangler" persona.

For example:

If you run a pediatrics practice...

Balance kids' needs to be entertained with parents' desire to keep them safe. For instance, be wary of germ-spreading toys, especially during flu season. Kids love stuffed animals but they are not very sanitary. Consider toys that are easily sanitized instead—and clean them daily. Better still, have a Disney movie playing on a loop in one corner. (Very few parents will object to *The Lion King* or *Frozen*, even if they've seen it a million times.)

Here's a clever idea we saw when we visited a pediatrics practice: The owner hired local artists and had giraffes painted all over one side of the practice and monkeys all over the other. Patients were in the Giraffe Wing or the Monkey Wing of the clinic. These themes carried through to the exam rooms as well: You were roomed in Giraffe 1, 2, 3, or 4 or Monkey 1, 2, 3, or 4 to wait for the clinician.

If you cater to older patients...

Follow their tastes, not your own. We worked with a GI doctor who had designed his practice in a stark neomodern style. We asked him, "How do your patients like this design?" He admitted, "Not all of them get it." So then we asked, "What's the average age of your patients?" He said, "Somewhere between 60 and 70." Aha! Neomodernism does not appeal to most people of this generation. This was a new doctor who had just gotten out of residency. He had designed the office to his tastes, not his patients'.

Likewise, when you're selecting music to play in your GI practice, you wouldn't choose a Top 20 mix. You'd choose more of a mellow blend of the '50s, '60s, and '70s. And you'd look for publications that appeal to the demographics of those patients, like maybe *AARP, Reader's Digest,* and *National Geographic.*

On the other hand…

If you cater to Millennials…

…you probably don't need to worry about magazines at all. They aren't relevant to this age group. What's important to this group of patients is that you provide Wi-Fi access and make sure they can recharge their devices in the reception area and in exam rooms. And don't ever make the mistake of trying to tell a Millennial she can't use her mobile phone while in your office—many of them will start to go into withdrawal after just a few minutes.

Finally, know that Millennials also want to be kept informed of what is going on. People in this age group are rarely willing to silently wait 30 minutes past their scheduled visit time without an update.

The point should be clear. Really think about the preferences of your patients as you create the right ambience for your practice. You want them to feel comfortable and welcome so that they'll keep coming back.

Processes and Technology

The mother of one of the authors of *Leading Medical Group Transformation* sent him a series of text messages that painfully illustrates the frustrating patient experience you create when processes and technology are sub-par. We've recreated it below:

- Doctor is referring me to a gynecological oncologist and says I should see them before I leave on the cruise in 2 weeks.
- Called the specialist office for an appointment, pushed option 1 as a new patient, waited on hold for 5 mins and then call was answered by someone who said they don't do scheduling for new patients and I needed to talk to Diane.
- Asked if they could transfer me to Diane and they said no, but if I hang up and call back in and push 1, I would get Diane. Explained I had done this and they said sorry but you need to try it again.
- Called back, pushed option 1 again. This time it rang and rang then it finally went to a call service who said they'd left for lunch, they'll be back at 2:00.

- Called back at 2:01, still on lunch, call service. Tried again at 2:07, pushed 1, got another lady who said Diane also does this, if you push 3, you'll actually get her for new patients, even though 3 is listed for med records.
- Called back, pushed 3, got Diane. Diane said, I do scheduling, but right now I'm not at my scheduling computer, so I'll have to call you back.
- Now 4:00, haven't heard anything back. Called the office and on-call is back activated.
- What do you think I should do?

Is this any way to treat a 70-year-old patient? Is this any way to treat a patient of *any* age? Of course not! And when you consider that this debacle occurred as the result of a referral to a gynecological oncology specialist—which is anxiety producing even when things go perfectly—it becomes even more of a cautionary tale. Make sure your processes and technology serve the patient's needs, not your own.

Now, let's compare this disaster with the experience the same patient had with the referring physician. The physician said, "I understand that you're getting ready to leave on a big cruise and that timing is really important. I will make sure I get your medical records together from today's visit. I'll send it over to the specialist and I'll also call her to let her know it's important you get in to see her in the next few days. If you come back here today before we close, I'll have the team pull together a full copy of your medical record and chart so it's ready to go with you."

This happened during a 10:00 a.m. appointment. The patient left, the doctor dictated the visit and got the chart generated, and the staff printed out and bundled everything. When the patient came back by his office at 4:30, the end of the day, the staff said to her, "We're all ready for you. Here's a full copy of your medical record and chart and lab tests and radiology! Please let us know if there's anything else we can do to help." (Note the contrast?)

If you're wondering how the story ended, here it is: The referring doctor ended up initiating a three-way call the next day using the doctor-to-doctor "secret" phone number and got her scheduled. Ironically, despite all the bureaucracy the specialist had put her through, she did end up having availability and scheduled the exam. Yet her referral processes and phone tree technology almost lost her a case.

Any female reader in particular can relate to how the author's mother must have felt. Imagine what it feels like to have a specialty referral to a gyneco-logical oncologist—the stress and anxiety already connected with that—and to have a terrible experience just trying to make an appointment. Don't put your patients through this!

Following are just a few of the points to consider regarding processes and technology. Make sure you are thinking about them from a patient-centric, patient-population standpoint and considering what they mean for your indi-vidual brand.

- Whether money is collected upfront or not
- How billing is handled
- How insurance processing is handled
- Collections procedures
- Whether you schedule referral appointments for patients or not
- How RFPs for vendors are handled
- How appointments are scheduled
- Coding and documentation
- Practice management system software
- EHR/how medical records are handled
- Whether you support patient portals
- Whether you support patient email interactions
- Whether you provide after-hours phone support

For example, if you're catering to Millennials in a major urban city, it's better to use technology and patient portals. It's better to support email and online scheduling. Yet if catering to "Greatest Generation" patients in rural Amer-ica, none of that matters. What matters is your phone support. These people really want to talk to a real live human being.

Hiring and Training the Right People

Even more important than the physical dimensions of your practice are the "people dimensions."

Focus groups reveal that it's not only the clinician patients like and are loyal to. It's the whole team. Patients are very sensitive to team turnover. They don't like it. All the more reason medical groups should strive to hire the right people and train them well.

Never forget that your brand is comprised mostly of your people. While your physical location, décor, and processes *do* matter, they're meaningless if the people who care for and interact with your patients aren't always friendly and engaging. Just like it's the baristas who provide the consistent coffee experience at Starbucks, it's the staff who will provide the consistent healthcare experience in your medical practice.

Culture-Centric Hiring

Simply put, hire employees who fit your image and resonate with your patients. This is especially true of the people who staff your front desks. Pediatricians should hire frontline staff who have a rapport with children, gerontologists should hire those who get along well with seniors, and so forth.

Hire for the brand and the culture. Yes, this means age groups, as we just mentioned, but it can also mean other demographic classifications. If you cater to upper class wealthy patients, you need to hire staff members who can relate to or at least connect with these people. The same is true if you have a high percentage of Medicaid patients or Spanish-speaking patients.

When veterinary offices are seeking to hire staff members, particularly front desk people, they often interview with a dog or cat in the room. This is a good way to make sure they hire people who like animals. Medical group leaders who treat humans can learn a lot from this technique!

Beyond hiring for brand and culture "fit," you definitely want to hire friendly, likeable employees. It is quite possible to test for people skills. If a candidate can't think on his feet or comes across as awkward—or worse, surly and unpleasant—during an interview, then you'll know you have the wrong person.

It's a good idea to use peer interviewing to ensure that you have the right candidate before you pull the proverbial trigger. We briefly discussed peer interviewing in the context of hiring leaders in Chapter 3. The same principles hold true for front desk people and other office staff. We will address peer interviewing in more detail in Chapter 9.

And please, please, please don't move people "up front" because the clinicians can't interact with them in the back. This happens all the time and it is a terrible idea.

Training to your Brand Experience

If you want a consistent patient (brand) experience, you must invest in training. Developing standard processes to train leaders, clinicians, and staff is a crucial first step, of course. Then, during onboarding and orientation, you can focus on making sure new team members are doing their part to provide a consistent patient experience.

If someone used to make coffee at McDonald's and goes to work for Starbucks, he can't just jump in and start doing things the McDonald's way. He has to get trained to the Starbucks brand standards first. The same is true for your medical practice. New hires need to learn the "right" way to do everything: how to check patients in, how to direct them to exam rooms, how to do service recovery. Nothing should be left to chance.

Onboarding Clinical Team Members

Quite often, medical groups skip new employee orientation for physicians and other clinicians. Or they send these professionals to a shorter version of the training than everyone else receives. Then they wonder why clinicians don't act like team members and hold themselves to the same standards we expect from others.

Fact is, physicians are leaders. They, more than anyone else, need to conform to the standards of your brand. If they don't, it's like going to Disney World and seeing that Mickey and Minnie behave differently from all the other cast members. We can't even imagine it because they are the brand leaders, right? Well, so are physicians. Where they lead, your organization's staff will follow—make sure it's the destination you want.

What you're doing is skill building. You're investing upfront in the skills needed to convey and advance your brand. Yet skill building isn't a "one and done" event. As patient needs change and new initiatives are adopted, you'll need to train people again. And again. And again.

Actually, any time you realize staff members are not helping create a patient-centric culture, you should first assume you have a skill problem. Once everyone is "skilled up," you'll be able to discern who might be suffering from lack of will (which is a much worse problem than lack of skill).

We worked with a health system that had rolled out a new method of clinician order entry: e-prescribing. Rather than writing a paper prescription, clinicians would order it electronically and send it to the pharmacy for the patient. So, we asked how it was going. At first we got a technical answer: 99.99 percent of all electronic orders were being transmitted to the pharmacy correctly and being accepted. From a systems standpoint, the rollout was going well.

But when we pressed further with "How is clinician utilization going?" the room got really quiet. It turned out only 10 percent of clinicians were using the new e-prescribing system—even though research showed it was superior in every way to paper prescribing (more accurate, more convenient, reduced the number of follow-up calls, etc.) *and* despite the fact that posters were plastered all over the practice walls advertising it.

The bottom line was that clinicians didn't like the new system. It changed their work flow and they simply weren't comfortable with it so they weren't doing it. So we asked, "How much training have you provided clinicians?" They responded: "Well, we sent them some emails and an instruction sheet and a visual on how to do it."

The problem was clear: Nobody had gone into the clinic to actually do real skill development with the most important members of the care team. And so we sent a trainer in to work on site with clinicians. We held "lunch and learns" and had the person stick around after the training to help them if they got stuck or had questions. There was also an online resource to help them.

Six months later, after rolling out the program, we looked back and found that 92 percent were now using e-prescribing.

The point is, paper scripts were normal for clinicians. They had been writing them for years and their system worked. They were comfortable with it. Patients were, too. So why *would* they change if what they were doing had always worked fine? They wouldn't—but it was *not* a will problem. It was a skill problem. They needed to be retrained and gain a new skill before they could live up to their system's new brand promise.

So...What Do Your Patients Think?

The chapter you've just read is all about creating an excellent brand experience for *your* patients. You know who they are, you have a pretty good idea about what makes them happy, and you certainly want to give them the best possible care. Yet in terms of knowing how well you are serving your patients, there is no substitute for asking them directly.

Never assume that you know the perception your patients have of you. Instead, make a point of asking them. One way to do this is to invite friends and family to be a part of your practice and give you honest feedback. Another is to institute a mystery shopper program.

One medical group leader we work with—Holly Adams at OU Physicians in Oklahoma City—has her own version of mystery shopping. At her staff meetings she will have someone call one of OU's clinics and ask if they can get an appointment. Because access is one of their critical focus areas, the team is checking to see how consistently accessible their clinics are. Do they answer the phone in the prescribed OU way? Can the caller get an appointment right away? If not, can she be quickly connected to a clinic that *can* see her?

Also, CG CAHPS surveys can be very helpful in assessing patient experience across a system as well as in a specific practice location. For example, the survey will tell you if patients perceive office staff to be courteous and friendly. If you have low scores system-wide in this area, you'll know you have a skill development problem. If the data shows that one clinic is significantly different from the others, you'll know to look closer at what's happening there.

One physician group we worked with consistently showed up in the bottom 10th percentile, across the board, in how well they were providing access to patients requesting appointments. Only one clinic stood out, and its score was in the 88th percentile. So we carefully examined the practices of that one clinic. What were they doing differently?

What we found was this: When a patient calls and the practice can't accommodate them, they call around themselves and find someone who *can* see the patient. They don't make the patient navigate the system. Here's what the practice leader told us: "If it were *my* family member who couldn't get an appointment, I wouldn't make them call our 800 number. I would call around to the other clinic managers personally until I found someone who could see them today. So I decided we should do the same thing for our patients."

This is a great example of how to ensure positive patient perceptions. It's also the ultimate test for your brand. *If your own mother needed care from your practice, would you trust your brand experience enough to let her go through the same processes as all the other patients?*

This is the question that one of our authors saw answered in a disappointing way with his mother's frustrating experience. And—as you may recall from Chapter 2—it's the question at the heart of Singapore's Changi General Hospital's mission.

Now, we'll leave you to answer it for yourself. We all have a mom. We all want the best for her. And we hope you can honestly say that your own practice is providing that level of care and service she deserves, without your having to make any special accommodations.

CHAPTER 8

The Art of Efficiency:
Balancing Quality and Cost-Effectiveness

"All stakeholders want U.S. healthcare to be about much more than money. For this vision to be realized, physicians and customers will need to collaborate in measuring efficiency and inspiring physicians' pursuit of lower-cost paths to the best clinical outcomes."
    —Arnold Milstein, MD, MPH, and Thomas H. Lee, MD, *The New England Journal of Medicine*

Efficiency is valuable *only* if the process or medical group that has achieved it is also effective. Running a medical group that achieves both aims is not easy. Effectiveness for a medical group means that the patient is seen at the right time, in the right place, by the right clinical resources, and at the right level of quality and cost.

At first glance, there seems to be an inherent contradiction in terms when applying "efficiency" to patient care. "Efficiency" is a "cold" word, while "care" is a warm, human one. Yet when we dig deeper, we see that efficiency and patient care are not only compatible but are actually dependent on each other. When we run efficient and effective medical groups, we are able to consistently provide better, safer care to more people. From our perspective, effective medical groups and their leaders have the desire for efficient operations supported by optimized automation hardwired into their "DNA."

Let's define our terms: What *is* practice efficiency? In a nutshell it's the outcome that occurs when physicians and staff function as a team built around the care needs of the patient to optimize the use of both patient and physician time while staying within defined revenue, cost, and quality standards. This definition holds whether the practice functions within a fee-for-service or value-based environment, although the value-based environment places a higher premium on efficiency and effectiveness. (One other point: Much of what a medical group needs in order to ensure efficiency is supported by automation. So, when working on this aspect of medical group performance and leadership, remember that IT optimization is a critical tool to achieve efficiency and effectiveness.)

In truth, most medical groups are straddling both service reimbursement worlds. They're working in a *mostly* fee-for-service reimbursement environment while developing or executing on plans to move to a value-based reimbursement environment. The value-based landscape is still evolving, but it looks a lot like the current environment with different areas of focus—i.e., better alignment with health system services like ancillaries and tighter patterns of patient referral to raise clinical quality and reduce clinical expense.

Needless to say, having to work in two reimbursement environments is a major source of systemic inefficiency. This is the paradox of the current healthcare environment: We require a different level and type of efficiency while working under two very different models of reimbursement that require different operating models to be efficient.

Simply put, traditional fee-for-service reimbursement rewards volume and pays in the form of discrete services to patients. On the other hand, value-based reimbursement still rewards volume but within the context of optimized resource use that creates quality as the main outcome and tends to pay in the form of risk-based payment for total care of patients.

Navigating this minefield is enough to make leaders want to tear their hair out. Yet we find there *is* a way to consistently work toward practice efficiency. It depends on following this formula:

The Practice Efficiency Formula
Quality/Outcome + Resource Use = Efficiency

In other words, practice efficiency can be defined *only* within the context of quality. If you're "efficient" but aren't providing quality care, it doesn't count. In this sense, quality can be defined as effectiveness. Any patient care operation that doesn't yield quality is ineffective and also inefficient. Any resources that are used to generate low-quality patient care results are wasted. A general rule of thumb is that current medical group and health system operations, whether clinical or administrative, have 30 percent of the resources dedicated to them lost as waste. Clearly, there is a good reason to focus on this issue.

The solution is for leaders to define a very concise set of "critical to quality" principles tied to practice efficiency and aligned with the above formula—then drive on to continuously improve in all of these areas. As reimbursement and therefore the major component of medical group revenue continues its move to a value-based payment mechanism, the need to carefully define, implement, and monitor appropriate quality and cost metrics is a critical component of efficiency.

There are certain predictable factors that go into making a practice efficient. We've identified eight of them and will discuss each one below. Bear in mind that there are three different "groupings" of physician practices—primary care, specialty care, and hospital-based—and all of them must account for each of the eight keys to efficiency. But because each of the three types are different, they must apply these keys in the way that makes sense for them.

Eight Keys for Achieving Practice Efficiency

The following list of "efficiency keys" should function almost like a dashboard. Ask yourself: *Where does my practice group land on these parameters?* Even if they're not all where you want them to be—they almost certainly won't be—you must pay attention to all eight of them.

EFFICIENCY KEY 1: Reduced Clinical and Administrative Variation. Allowing high levels of variation to exist in both of these areas only confuses and frustrates patients and creates unnecessary expenses. It's important that you do everything in a consistent way for every patient across every practice in your system (not just your specific medical group)—from your hours of operation, to how you check in patients, to how you handle charting, to how you check blood pressure and take vital signs, to how you refer patients to other practices.

Starting at the most basic level, variation can be addressed with a set of common policies and processes that covers everything from hours of operation to work standards for all staff. This is essential to create efficiency. In an Oregon practice we worked with, the way patients checked in with Dr. Smith was completely different from the way they checked in with Dr. Jones. These were meaningless differences yet they have the potential to create real problems. For example, what happens when the person at the front desk who knows both doctors' preferences is out sick one day? Whoever has to fill in probably doesn't know these differences and will be completely hamstrung. So the practice has to overstaff to cover this scenario.

Clinical variation also takes a toll on efficiency. We worked with an orthopedic practice in Colorado that had no common protocol for broken wrists even though they treated at least 60 in a two-month period (ski injuries). All of the physicians did every step differently. They needed to develop a consensus on how to handle all clinical processes: *Who would see the patient first? How would she get the patient ready to see the physician? What would the physician do? After they pinned or cast the patient, how would the handover happen?*

To solve this problem, the practice started working toward clinical consistency on a number of fronts. Chief among them is a relatively aggressive move toward joining an independent practice association that in turn will be part of a regional clinically integrated network. The concept being that through this path they will have a common medical record, common patient care handovers, and consistent data on patient care outcomes and therefore quality.

On the other hand, the Missouri Orthopaedic Institute at the University of Missouri-Columbia treats its patients' broken wrists with incredible consistency. A single surgeon who can no longer do surgery performs the initial evaluation. He figures out the treatment protocol and passes the patient along to one of 30 orthopedic surgeons. All 30 surgeons then handle their processes exactly the same way. Repetition leads to improvement. Everyone gets better and better at what they do. Overall clinical quality rises, engagement goes up, and the patient experience improves.

One often overlooked but critical factor to address while improving the amount of variation that exists is to ensure that documentation of patient care services (a.k.a. coding) is performed by trained and qualified people. Traditionally coding and documentation have focused on reimbursement needs for the revenue cycle but increasingly they are critical for understanding variation and also defining and addressing quality and variance from your quality standards.

Here's the bottom line: Physicians need to come together to hammer out some basic policies to make common across the practice. Don't "tell" physicians what they should all be doing. Rather, ask them and let them come up with their own solutions. Physicians appreciate standardization and consistency. When they understand there is a better way to do things, and when they have a hand in crafting the solution, they will happily adopt it.

EFFICIENCY KEY 2: A Standardized Medical Group Staffing Model Tied to Your Practice Specialty Type. The first rule is simple: don't understaff. That's the biggest mistake practices make, and inappropriate staffing by definition creates inefficiency and ineffectiveness. Organizations tend to think in terms of what they can afford at the moment. This is understandable, but it's kind of a "chicken or egg" problem. If you don't staff properly, you'll never have the financial wherewithal to be able to staff properly. It's an endless cycle.

The other common error is to staff ambulatory practice sites on a fixed staffing model without regard to patient volume. This often leads to "bare minimum" staffing as leaders seek to level out expense across all clinical and business hours. Finding the balance between patient demand and provider capacity is an important area of focus in order to get the right staffing level in place to ensure efficient and effective care that in turn drives high patient engagement.

Highlighting this area of efficiency is an article published in the *Annals of Family Medicine* that measures primary care staffing levels. The writers found that staffing patterns for primary care practices in the Centers for Medicare and Medicaid Services (CMS) Comprehensive Primary Care (CPC) initiative were marked by the following staffing characteristics:

"...At baseline, most CPC initiative practices used traditional staffing models and did not report having dedicated staff who may be integral to new primary care models, such as care coordinators, health educators, behavioral health specialists, and pharmacists. Without such staff and payment for their services, practices are unlikely to deliver comprehensive, coordinated, and accessible care to patients at a sustainable cost."

Oddly, common benchmarks for medical group staffing levels have traditionally been highly variable and a "correct ratio" that can be used as a common standard has been shrouded in mystery. The study helps clear this mystery up although there is still considerable variation that exists based on practice setting. The article continues:

"Among all CPC primary care initiative medical groups, the ratio of all FTE staff to FTE physician is 4.50 (2.49 are non-administrative staff, and 2.01 are administrative staff). The Medical Group Management Association reported that nationwide, internal medicine practices owned by a hospital or integrated delivery system reported 2.68 FTE staff per FTE physician in 2009. This benchmark is different from that of the CPC initiative sample, as just less than one-half of CPC initiative practices are owned by a larger organization. The staffing ratio among CPC initiative practices falls from a ratio of 5.32 among the smallest practices to 3.35 for the largest."[1]

This suggests that larger practices gain efficiency by centralizing certain services that smaller medical groups are unable to centralize. The study also finds that a model that improves efficiency for primary care delivery in a value-based reimbursement model—the patient-centered medical home (PCMH)—requires little difference in staffing between practices with and without them. This is interesting as it has been suggested that PCMH models, while clinically effective, need additional staff. The study suggests that, potentially, the only difference in staffing is created by the type of FTE rather than the raw numbers.

What does all this mean? First, the larger message is that benchmarks continue to be of limited value for determining specific staffing levels beyond serving as a directional guide. Each medical group must develop its own plan to address patient care that takes into account an appropriate mix of clinical and administrative staff working as a team to address patient care needs in a timely and efficient manner.

Second, there needs to be the right mix of staff members (clinical and administrative), and they need to be able to work at the top of their capability and licensure within an optimized flow of patient care. This allows the clinical team to focus on being available for the patient at the right time with the right level of clinical resources.

Third, physicians need to work with the staff as a real team member. The simplest example is to highlight an important aspect of a medical assistant's (MA) role in the care team: reviewing and triaging ancillary test results rather than having the physician, APP, or RN nursing staff do this. The MA can quickly bring important information to the attention of the nursing team, pharmacists, and the physician. This allows these higher-level clinical resources to focus on timely communication with the patient in a way that engages her and to deliver the right type of care in a way that optimizes efficiency and effectiveness.

Of course, staffing ratios aside, you have to hire quality people who can work together as a team and are really able to serve the patient. As we've discussed elsewhere in this book, peer interviewing using behavioral-based interview techniques can help ensure a good hire. (To learn more, visit www.studergroup.com/medical-group/peer-interviewing.) Just be aware that you can turn a high-performing employee into an ineffective employee if you give her too many things to do.

By the way, be sure you aren't hiring *only* for efficiency. It's also critical that employees have a high degree of situational empathy and understanding of patient issues and needs. We visited one ENT practice with a front desk staffer who clearly struggles to connect with its two different types of patients: frightened parents and older people with hearing problems. She's efficient, sure, but she doesn't know how to engage with patients. It's really important to have both.

EFFICIENCY KEY 3: A Team-Based Operations Approach with All Team Members Working at the Top of Their Competency and Licensure. As mentioned earlier, it's important to work as a team so the physician isn't the only person doing everything. The question practice managers and/or physician leaders need to continue to ask about medical group operations is if the right work is assigned to the right people. It's also important to do sufficient rounding on those critical staff (a.k.a. physicians, nurses, medical assistants, clinical supervisors, etc.) to make sure that the work flow and supporting information systems are properly optimized and that there is as little wasted effort and time as is reasonable at every level of the organization. This of course needs to be backed up with metrics that either support or otherwise clarify what you hear during rounding.

To achieve these goals, leaders must be wired with an efficiency mindset. You can tell you have this mindset baked into your organization if the practice leadership team a) routinely works with and supports frontline staff and b) does structured reviews of every patient care process and every step of that process to make improvements that demonstrate results as measured by your metrics and key performance indicators. It isn't OCD. It is a basic management skill.

EFFICIENCY KEY 4: Well-Designed Facilities Layout and Operations Models. The way you design and optimize the facilities used by your medical group really matters. For example, it's important to address parking, signage, and placement of services in a logical configuration that supports the flow of patients and team members through the facility. If you are a primary care practice, the MGMA annual cost survey suggests that an experienced provider requires approximately 1,900 square feet of active clinical practice space. That translates to two or three exam rooms per provider and presumes that during a normal work week, each provider will see around 20-25 patients per day. We suggest you take the time to do the math, closely review the area, and optimize the provider's support staff and work flow to get to what is right for you. Once you do this, you will have removed a major barrier to efficiency.

Individual medical specialties have their own unique needs for exam rooms and these depend heavily on the age, acuity, and type of clinical service provided. Many practices make big mistakes in purchasing or designing facilities and don't realize them until later because they didn't take the time upfront to really dig into the specific needs of the patients, providers, and specialty type. This is not rocket science. It's something you address by working closely with the clinical staff and a knowledgeable architect (if you can) and by doing the math and operations efficiency study to achieve workable flow.

We worked with a neurology practice in Kansas that served many Parkinson's disease patients. They put the clinic on an inside corridor of the building and thought it was a great placement because it allowed physicians to be close to their testing lab. Unfortunately, it was terrible for patients, for two reasons. One, the location was a long way from the parking lot and required negotiating multiple doorways. Parkinson's patients often have problems with walking and changing stride to move through doors. Two, the main clinic entrance didn't have automatic doors. Both problems made for a very unfriendly and difficult experience just trying to get to the office, let alone to see the neurology team.

The moral of the story? Take a good look at who your patients are and ensure that your facility makes sense for their needs. Try to anticipate changes that might happen in the future as well. The Orthopaedic Institute we discussed earlier is a prime example. When they initially designed their clinic space, they didn't realize they'd have patients showing up on gurneys, yet it happened. Though their hallways were set to standard and met all code requirements, they weren't wide enough to accommodate the gurneys and so they ended up having to modify the space and rethink patient transport requirements.

It can be really expensive to make changes to your physical environment. We worked with a California health system that opened a new hospital. When they were moving their clinic spaces, they had to change a door. Because of the Office of Statewide Health Planning and Development (OSHPD), the regulatory agency that controls healthcare facilities in California, moving the door ended up being a $250,000 proposition. Therefore, take the time to carefully evaluate, maybe even simulate, your facility corridors, exam rooms, location of ancillaries, parking lots, signage, and any other important aspects of your physical plant to prevent and remove these potential barriers to efficiency.

EFFICIENCY KEY 5: Optimized EHR and Practice Management IT Platform Work Flow. This one almost goes without saying, now that the electronic health record (EHR) has moved into the ambulatory space. Probably 60 to 75 percent of everything your team does, both clinical and administrative, is driven by some sort of automated tool. For practice efficiency, you must ensure that your electronic health record and other technology are integrated into your workflow.

The EHR design and its incompatibility with efficient workflow have been widely commented on in the press. And deservedly so. Too often, the needs of clinicians are overlooked, and a tool that should potentially serve as a boost to efficiency becomes a drag on efficiency instead. To provide a simple example, many prominent EHR products tend to send all ancillary service results only to physicians. This is logical but impractical. As mentioned in Keys 2 and 3, a high-functioning clinical medical assistant can triage results for the physician and therefore reduce workload. The EHR design must also match this approach.

EHR installation design that triggers all clinical work flow off a decision by the physician rather than distributing work load to the right clinical resource is therefore a major culprit of inefficiency. This design, along with the way critical patient data is captured and stored, should be a key area of focus by management in order to improve efficiency and patient care. We recommend a standardized review process designed to ferret out poorly tailored or customized EHR and practice management software. This is an issue with all of the leading EHR software products on the market and leads to what physicians call "death by 1,000 clicks." It is not a new phenomenon but given that clinical work flow has now become automated, the problem is impacting patient care efficiency and therefore quality and patient engagement.

EFFICIENCY KEY 6: Well-Defined Quality and Engagement Metrics with Aligned Metrics and Tools. There's a mature body of quality and engagement metrics for acute care settings. Yet for most medical groups, this is still very much an emerging area. We need to spend as much time defining and refining our quality metrics as we do our revenue cycle and other operations metrics. (Once again, efficiency without quality doesn't count.)

Clinician and Group Consumer Assessment of Healthcare Providers and Systems (CG CAHPS) is the leading tool as of now for tracking and reporting on where a practice stands in clinical quality, safety, and evidence-based medicine. In a nutshell, CG CAHPS is a family of surveys that measure patients' perception of care given by physicians and other providers in an office setting. A good amount of research suggests that patient experience and quality are two sides of the same coin.

To learn more about CG CAHPS, we invite you to read *The CG CAHPS Handbook: A Guide to Improve Patient Experience and Clinical Outcomes*, by Jeff Morris, MD, MBA, FACS; Barbara Hotko, RN, MPA; and Matthew Bates, MPH. This book not only provides proven tactics broken down by CG CAHPS composite, it offers up plenty of evidence that when you improve the patient experience, clinical quality also improves. To read more, please visit www.firestarterpublishing.com/cgcahps.

Consider the following excerpt:

Patient experience is positively correlated with better health outcomes. In one study, patient's perception of care was found to be directly linked to improved blood sugar control in diabetic patients. In another study, positive primary care follow-up was found to offset poor hospital experience and outcomes.[2]

Reporting on quality metrics as more of an inherent component of daily clinical practice and sharing this data with peers, the health system, payers, and regulators is relatively new to many medical groups. It is one of the most fundamental and dramatic changes to ambulatory medicine. The nature of quality and performance reporting has also changed. Up until 2017, most reporting has been of the yes/no variety. There is a real need (and a growing requirement) now for medical groups to move to a more quantitative tracking and reporting approach—one that demonstrates to patients and payers that you actually do provide higher quality at a lower cost. In fact, reimbursement models like the CMS Quality Payment Program and MIPS will require this.

Medical groups need to develop an operations, financial, and information system infrastructure that allows them to accept the financial risk necessary for participating in payer reimbursement models that require them to manage the majority of the care for a set number of patients. This is not really a new concept. It's just that now there is a great deal more focus on and capability for collecting and reporting data at the physician and provider level in order to drive improvements in quality and reduce excess cost from the healthcare process. Every medical group needs to rapidly move toward collecting, managing, and understanding quality data in a way that can help them demonstrate quality.

EFFICIENCY KEY 7: Well-Defined Team Compensation Goals and Models (Providers and Administrators). Quite simply, people's performance reflects the way they're paid. This means your medical practice has to follow a reasonable compensation model for providers, administrators, nurses, and all employees. Otherwise they won't be high performers, and, eventually, they'll leave for better-paying positions. (Of course, you don't want to overpay, either.)

Traditionally, provider compensation has been structured to reward volume. We now need an approach that recognizes efficiency and effectiveness *within the context* of volume—with value being even more important.

It's also crucial to embrace a physician compensation framework that incentivizes while also integrating providers with each other and with the system. To learn more, we invite you to read Huron's white paper *Change Behavior,*

Prevent Burnout, and Still Transform to Value-Based Care: Rethinking Physician Compensation at www.studergroup.com/medical-group.

Be careful about advanced practice provider, nursing, and other clinical staff compensation, too. Many health systems fall into the trap of paying clinical staff the same across the board—whether they're working in an inpatient acute care setting or in an ambulatory setting. In fact, these are radically different jobs and should be paid at different levels.

When compensating staff, be sure to pay local market rates—not just health-care market rates. When Vic Arnold worked at a healthcare organization in Kansas City, he found that leaders weren't taking into account the local casino employment market. Essentially, casinos were wooing employees such as registration clerks to leave because they paid $2 an hour higher for very similar jobs. Obviously, the resulting high turnover rates weren't helping efficiency.

EFFICIENCY KEY 8: Timely Patient Access (Beyond Efficient Appointment Scheduling). In this context *access* means the ready availability of care to patients in multiple formats and locations. Medical groups need to create an "access points strategy" aimed at meeting patient needs across all settings while ensuring strong care coordination support across the many points of handover that constitute the continuum of care. In a primary care or specialty practice context this may include:

- Traditional clinic/office setting
- Urgent care
- Retail care
- Telehealth, mHealth, and eHealth access

Each of the above sites must develop well-coordinated processes for accepting patients and appropriately managing patient needs. These include:

- Well-coordinated work hours and appointment types.
- Consistent and easy-to-understand provider schedules and appointments.
- Clear communication about care needs and delivery, including pre- and post-care support.

- Transfer and referral work flow that supports care coordination. Note that this includes the ability to manage "outbound" and "inbound" referrals for patients in a timely manner and in such a way that care quality is not compromised. It's also important not to create financial burdens on patients by sending them to providers that are not part of your medical group's and related payers' network while still ensuring quality care (as demonstrated by longitudinal clinical outcome).
- EHR and practice management software that clearly documents and helps coordinate access.

These well-coordinated processes also apply to other care sites and types. It all should be seamless to patients so they and their families have a simple and high-quality experience.

It's also important for both primary care and specialty care sites to provide patients with easy access to pharmacies as well as appropriate ancillary services such as radiology, pathology/lab, physical therapy, and occupational therapy. This includes access to timely results and consultations as necessary.

Efficient cross scheduling of ancillary services is a big issue. A hospital client once told us that even though they have three well-located ancillary sites for radiology services, the medical groups are all scheduling patients to one site over the other two sites for no obvious reason. This creates a bottleneck and a resource problem that ends up delaying needed care for some patients. This organization needs to take steps to ensure that there is easy and balanced access to radiology lab services by location.

The more of these efficiency keys you perfect, the more effective your care will become and the higher your patient and staff engagement levels will be. This consistency will make everyone happier as well as improve quality and your need to demonstrate value.

Now, let's take a brief look at specific things each of the three types of medical groups—primary care, specialty care, and hospital-based—can do to become more efficient.

Primary Care Practices: Consider Becoming a Patient-Centered Medical Home

Primary care practices are the "backbone" of the United States healthcare system and a key starting point for medical groups to be more effective and efficient. The Institute of Medicine's definition of primary care is the following: "Primary care is the provision of integrated, accessible healthcare services by clinicians who are accountable for addressing a large majority of personal healthcare needs, developing a sustained partnership with patients, and practicing in the context of family and community." So, primary care is the place where the majority of the care patients need should be provided, rather than in more expensive and often less clinically effective Emergency Departments, urgent care sites, or even via specialty care providers.

The providers whose medical practice approach meets the definition of primary care are a relatively broad group of physicians and often include family practice, general internal medicine, pediatrics, and even OB/GYN physicians. Historically, primary care practices focused on traditional fee-for-service, illness-oriented, physician-centric practice models that fell far short of the Triple Aim of healthcare that is driving organizations to embrace a more patient-centered and value-driven model. At present, the main tool for creating efficiency and effectiveness for primary care medical groups is the patient-centered medical home (PCMH).

The PCMH model is designed to help primary care practices become more efficient by creating more effective and predictable outcomes over the course of a patient's interaction with the health system. It places an emphasis on having clinical and administrative staff work as a true team to manage patients over the long term in order to care for them in a more standardized and streamlined way. This is the framework that allows a health system to deploy the Huron Chips & Bricks SM strategy we discussed back in Chapter 5.

A PCMH offers the following benefits:
- **Physician-Led Practice.** Patients have access to a personal physician who leads the care team within a medical practice.

- **Whole-Person Orientation.** The care team provides comprehensive care, including acute care, chronic care, preventive services, and end-of-life care, at all stages of life.
- **Integrated and Coordinated Care.** Practices take steps to ensure that patients receive the care and services they need from the medical neighborhood in a culturally and linguistically appropriate manner.
- **Focus on Quality and Safety.** Practices use the quality improvement process and evidence-based medicine to continually improve patient outcomes.
- **Access.** Practices commit to enhancing patients' access to care.[3]

When you look at all of these items, you can clearly see that this is not the "Physician Father Knows Best" approach we associate with traditional primary care. The emphasis of the PCMH model is to focus on the patient and to provide efficient and effective care as defined earlier in this chapter. While published and peer reviewed academic studies of PCMH outcomes are still being developed, early experiences with this model in our consulting practice have shown this model to be a practical, efficient, and effective way to improve patients' perceptions of care as well as *actual* care.

Specialty Care Practices: Take Steps to Reduce Variations in Processes and Handovers

There is a specialty medical home model too. However, we have not seen it in our consulting practice as frequently as we have seen the primary care PCMH. It's built on the PCMH foundation and adds these features to ensure efficiency and quality:

- Written referral agreements on specialists' roles and responsibilities and expectations for sharing information and coordinating care
- Standards for timely access to care and clinical advice based on patient need
- A systematic approach to track patients and coordinate care
- Measuring performance to identify and act on needed improvements[4]

While we strongly recommend the PCMH model for primary care, we don't see it as a "must do" for specialty practices. There are other ways they can, and should, improve efficiency.

Specialty practices have a similar staffing approach as primary care. Typically, however, the APPs (physician assistants and nurse practitioners) and various clinical nursing and allied health specialties are more actively involved in the practice and work in more of a team-based arrangement. They are more directly tied to specialists than are their primary care counterparts and "own" key components of the patient care process. They may help specialists determine true clinical need for specialist services, provide routine follow-up after a procedure, etc. Therefore the administrative and clinical staffing model tends to follow the specialty practice model; ophthalmologists have technicians, otolaryngologists have audiologists, oncologists use ARNPs to triage and follow patients through treatment cycles, and so forth.

Each type of specialty practice has a very specific way of managing patients and providing team-based care. For example:

If you're an oncology practice, when your patient comes in she has often already been diagnosed and referred by a primary care physician to the practice. An APP may first evaluate the case to help develop the treatment plan. Notification of the diagnosis and a request to initiate treatment to an insurance payer is a critical first step. This step is important to ensure that there is minimal delay in treatment for the patient, given the need for timely care.

If the decision is to start with chemotherapy, a medical oncologist will take the patient's case and develop a plan of care. For the first and subsequent treatments, after she walks in the door of the medical oncology practice, she has labs drawn to make sure she is able to accept the chemotherapy that's been prescribed. Then she'll see a practitioner who actually mixes the chemotherapy drugs, assists her into an infusion chair, and administers the treatment. Then she will see the oncologist on a timely basis to receive feedback on her care and to answer questions, plan next steps, and so forth.

If you're a surgical oncology practice, your patient may also be referred to first see a PA or nurse practitioner who evaluates her and identifies possible protocols and works with the surgeon to determine the right course of care that ties in with the medical oncologist's work and the overall patient plan. Then she will see the surgeon who makes a decision about surgery. Then she will be referred to the hospital. The next time the patient comes to your practice will be for post-surgical care and to work with the overall care team to determine if there are further protocols to follow. In this way, the clinicians work as a team to care for the patient's needs and to ensure that the appropriate handovers occur efficiently and in a timely fashion.

For specialists, efficiency is as much about how well you coordinate with the referring physician (often a primary care physician) and execute diagnostic processes and handovers from one team member to another as it is about the actual procedure that is performed by the specialist (so long as all are completed effectively). To ensure quality, it is important that specialty practices follow some version of a plan, do, check, act methodology—taking these prescribed steps to ensure their work flow is optimized and their care is effective. Our suggestion here is to take your efforts to the next level—take the time to understand and make active changes to make this aspect of your medical group more efficient and built around the needs of patients.

Hospital-Based Physicians: Integrate Appropriately Within the Health System at the Acute Care and Medical Group Levels

A hospital-based physician (HBP) is exactly what the name states: a physician whose professional activities are performed chiefly within a hospital setting. Some examples are hospitalists, anesthesiologists, Emergency Department physicians, intensivists (intensive care specialists—typically pulmonologists by specialty), pathologists, and radiologists. While a few of them have ambulatory practice operations, most do not. Their efficiency is tied to the treatment of acutely ill patients they care for in an inpatient setting. Their practice operations, quality measures, and efficiency have a direct impact on quality and cost for a health system and the system's medical group.

Handovers are an important aspect of the work of hospital-based physicians, just as they are for the rest of the care team. In fact, one of the keys to practice efficiency in this area is how well the primary care and specialty care physicians hand over patient care to the hospital-based physicians and vice versa. These handovers are critical to quality and efficiency and are watched closely under most value-based reimbursement contracts in terms of performance monitoring and scoring of quality performance. At the core of a good handover is communication, whether you're moving a patient from the ED setting to an acute care bed or performing patient discharge activities. At every step, crisp and timely communication is a key to efficiency.

Another area of importance is that the hospital-based physicians need to have a formal and direct relationship with the other members of the medical group associated with the health system. This is true even if some or all of these HBP services are outsourced. Frequent interactions focused on individual patient care issues and more global clinical quality and efficiency matters are critical to success.

Here's the takeaway: Whichever type of practice you lead, efficiency and effectiveness really matter. Take a hard look at the eight keys to efficiency and see where you most need to make changes. We were struck by a commentary put out by the National Committee for Quality Assurance (NCQA) on this topic, and it's important to consider as a medical group takes steps to transform itself:

"The words *efficiency* and *effectiveness* are often considered synonyms, along with terms like *competency, productivity,* and *proficiency*. However, in more formal management discussions, the words *efficiency* and *effectiveness* take on very different meanings. In the context of process reengineering, Lon Roberts (1994: 19) defines efficiency as 'to the degree of economy with which the process consumes resources—especially time and money,' while he distinguishes effectiveness as 'how well the process actually accomplishes its intended purpose, here again from the customer's point of view.'" (Remember, for our purposes "customer" – "patient.")[5]

So, the more efficient your practice is, the more patients you can serve and the better you can serve them. Efficiency helps you live your mission. Once efficiency has been established, then the more effective your medical group will be in addressing patient needs—and therefore it will also be more capable of succeeding with the transformation of the market. Don't underestimate its importance as you move toward excellence.

CHAPTER 9

Creating a Culture of High Engagement

"When people are financially invested, they want a return. When people are emotionally invested, they want to con-tribute."
—Simon Sinek, Author of *Start with Why*

"Patient engagement is the blockbuster drug of the century."
—Dr. Farzad Mostashari, Former National Coordinator for Health Information Technology

"Patients do not put their trust in machines or devices. They put their trust in you."
—Dr. Margaret Hamburg, Former Commissioner of the U.S. Food & Drug Administration (FDA)

Matthew, one of the authors of this book, was eating dinner with a health system chief medical officer (CMO) and his wife. The CMO had recently retired from his leadership role where he was responsible for a multispecialty medical group, a hospital, and multiple outpatient facilities. His wife told us a story that to us perfectly illustrates what engagement looks like in action.

Back when the CMO—we'll call him Thomas—was a new Emergency Department doctor, he was working on Christmas Eve. He was supposed to get home in time to celebrate Christmas Day with his wife and their young children. But as so often happens when you work in the ED, the best-laid plans have a way of crumbling. A multi-vehicle, multi-patient auto accident required Thomas to stay at the hospital well into Christmas Day—eight hours after his shift was supposed to end.

The health system CEO learned what was going on and showed up at Thomas's house with presents for his kids. He said, "I'm so sorry your dad isn't home with you today. He misses you and wants to be here but he is busy saving lives." When Thomas called home to apologize for not being there on Christmas Day, he was sure his wife would be aggravated. But the CEO's visit had gone a long way toward helping put her husband's absence in perspective. She said gently, "It's okay. We love and support you."

When he got home late in the day, Thomas learned what the CEO had done. And despite his exhaustion from the endless gut-wrenching hours he had just put in, he was deeply touched. If it were possible to pinpoint a "moment of engagement," this was his.

As it turned out, Thomas stayed with the health system for 22 years. At his retirement party, he shared the story you've just read. His wife and kids remembered that Christmas Day very well. They got tears in their eyes as they realized how much he had always appreciated their support and understanding and how devoted he was to the patients whose lives he had always held in his hands.

Yes, it's a heartwarming story. But it's also a great illustration of how we in healthcare harvest what we plant. By going out of his way to engage this new ED doctor, that CEO ended up harvesting 20-plus years of dividends. Thomas had "paid it forward" to his organization, his patients, and his community over the years.

Oh, and here's the kicker: After Thomas retired, he came back "part-time," working three or four shifts per week in the ED! These are the fruits of engagement.

Our colleague Craig Deao, a senior leader at Studer Group®, has just written a book called *The E-Factor: How Engaged Patients, Clinicians, Leaders, and Employees Will Transform Healthcare*. Much of the information in this chapter was inspired by this book. Here is how Deao describes engagement:

While satisfaction is a one-way street ("What's the organization doing for me? What do I get?"), engagement is a two-way street ("How are we partnering together to create value?"). It's about giving discretionary effort, even when no one is watching. It's about tapping into that reservoir to decide if I—as an employee, a clinician, or a patient—will decide to take a specific action or not. Engagement means closing the "knowing-doing" gap so that a person has more than the right plan...they actually get it done.[1]

Every medical group should have a culture built around engagement. Everyone should be engaged—leaders, clinicians, employees, and, most of all, patients.

Why Engagement Is Everything

Engagement matters because it leads to better patient care. Great clinical quality depends on it. So does maximizing reimbursement. When team members and patients aren't engaged, bad things happen. Turnover increases. Physicians burn out. Patients don't comply with their care plans and may end up getting sicker.

On the other hand, when an organization *does* have a culture of engagement, all of these problems are less likely to occur. And the good news is that most people want to be fully engaged in their work—*especially* when that work centers on improving and even saving the lives of others.

Consider this wording that appeared on signs posted in a hospital: **"Hand hygiene prevents patients from catching diseases."** A peer-reviewed study found this sign created the highest hand-washing compliance rate as compared to wording that substituted "you" for "patients."[2] Apparently, the prospect of personal consequences isn't nearly as motivating as the desire to protect the health of patients.

This study tells us a lot about the nature of engagement. Real engagement in our work—doing the right thing even when no one is watching—happens when we are able to connect to our *why* at a human, emotional level. It's about the impact we have on others, not ourselves. This is what keeps us in our jobs, doing what we do despite the trials and tribulations that come with this work.

Healthcare professionals believe in what they do for a living. People don't choose a career in healthcare because it's the easiest way to make a good living. You can make money in healthcare, yes, but there are plenty of trade-offs: many years of schooling, hundreds of thousands of dollars of debt, long hours of difficult work (often on holidays). You go into healthcare because you want to make a difference in people's lives.

As you'll recall from Chapter 3, "purpose, worthwhile work, and making a difference" are the core values that drive healthcare professionals and keep them motivated. To keep people engaged, leaders need to constantly reconnect them with these values and reinforce the outcomes that result.

Speaking of leaders, they're the other factor that keeps us engaged. We need to trust our leaders. Here's a quick exercise to try: How would you complete this sentence?

The best boss I ever had was_____[fill in the name] because she _____[fill in the reason].

Odds are really high that you picked a "human" reason. When we ask people to do this exercise, we find that words like *caring, honesty,* and *open communication* tend to come up. They tend *not* to pick words like *smartest, most skilled, best educated,* or even *most fun.*

Matthew once worked inside a medical group where the CEO made a major restructuring announcement. The CEO then visited all the clinic locations. It took him three weeks and required him to cancel other commitments. He did it because he wanted clinicians and employees to understand why they were restructuring and to know that he cared about how it made them feel. ("I still wonder to this day where he vented all the anger and angst he received during those three weeks," says Matthew.)

Besides being empathetic and caring, leaders need to use language that portrays them as human beings, not corporate automatons. In Matthew's first C-suite role, one of the vice-presidents who reported to him left him a voice mail saying his first all-staff email was "crap." He reread the email and discovered she was right. By the time his colleagues in HR, legal, and communications had ensured the message was accurate and press-proof, it had been stripped of any humanity or personality.

In today's transforming healthcare environment, there is no more room for robotic emails or robotic anything else. Leaders *have* to be fully engaged and *have* to be able to engage the other stakeholders as well. Creating and maintaining engagement are no longer optional. It's no longer the secret sauce. It's now one of the key defining items that determine an organization's success or failure.

How Engagement Flows Through Your Organization

Engagement must exist at all levels of your organization. It can't be a list of "to-dos." It's not just about change but about transformation. Therefore it must be viewed as a comprehensive strategy that impacts leaders, clinicians, employees, and patients.

We have developed a four-pronged engagement model that helps organizations engage all four groups simultaneously. As you can see below, engaged leaders allow clinicians and employees to become engaged. In turn, these groups commit to the type of patient interactions that get patients engaged in their own care.

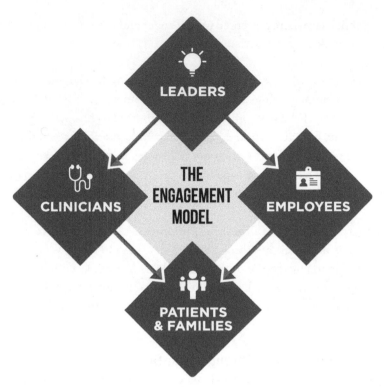

Figure 9.1 | Engagement Flows from Leaders to Clinicians and Employees and Then to Patients and Families

This model holds true for all kinds of practices. Whether you're affiliated with a larger health system, are part of a large medical group, or are a standalone practice, engagement must begin with your leaders.

Job 1: Getting Leaders Engaged

First things first: Who *is* a leader? The answer is really simple: If others follow you, then you're a leader. Sometimes organizations get confused and think leaders are only those individuals defined as such by an organization chart. In our experience, some of the most influential leaders in organizations don't carry big formal titles. (Conversely there are some "leaders" on the organization chart who have no followers. Sad but true.)

Perhaps the best example of an "unofficial" leader is the clinician whose advice people seek out when they need clinical guidance. Often in a practice there is one particular physician everyone calls when their child is sick or their mother needs surgery. You know the one. This person may or may not be labeled "leader" on the organization chart. Nonetheless, he *is* a clinical leader.

Leaders fall on both sides of the dyad. We know more than one financial leader who has been known to help her physician colleagues with personal financial questions.

Regardless of their status, official or unofficial, your leaders need to be engaged. If they're not, you'll find that engagement problems persist across all the other stakeholder groups as well. Conversely, organizations with highly engaged leaders will have engaged clinicians, staff, and patients. The CEO we talked about at the beginning of this chapter is a good example; he was engaged and thus he was able to engage others on the team.

This is where things can get tough. Leadership engagement does not happen based on what we talk about; it's based on what we do—our actions. As leaders we need to ensure that we, ourselves, are engaged and that the leaders who report to us are too. Quint Studer—founder of Studer Group and a thought leader in healthcare for more than 30 years—used to remind us that "what we permit we promote." We think this advice is as pertinent today as it has ever been. Let us illustrate it for you:

We once worked with a physician organization where a medical practice had been acquired by a health system and everyone was guaranteed their job for the next three years. Unfortunately, the practice manager who had been with the practice for over 20 years was "checked out." She was a nice person and was good at the social events, but in regard to making changes to adapt to system standards, she was just not interested in participating. Rather than openly disagree with the system policies, she started hanging out in her office and ignoring them.

When we first met her, she told us, "I'm just too old to change or to fight with the 'system.' I just need to work two more years to get my daughter through college and then I can retire. And besides, if one of those system policies is a really big deal, I'm sure someone will tell me and give me time to change before they take any drastic action."

So we worked with leadership to hold her accountable, and we're pleased to share that the story had a good ending. After a few months of senior leadership regularly visiting the practice, she reengaged and decided she was not too old to change. This change of heart is a direct result of the engagement of the leadership team and their commitment to knowing what was important to the practice manager and what was needed to get the desired outcomes. In fact, when we last visited her practice, hers was one of the highest performing across the system of more than 100 clinics.

The takeaway for leaders? It's never too late to get engaged and start having a positive impact on your organization. No one is a lost cause.

Engaging Physicians

Engagement is an antidote to physician burnout. And this problem is much more serious than many people realize. In his book *Healing Physician Burnout*, Quint Studer notes that 30 to 65 percent of physicians are burned out.[3] A Mayo clinic study conducted in 2014 with 6,880 physician respondents found similar results: 54.4 percent of physicians reported at least one sign of burnout.[4]

Why is clinician burnout such a serious issue? There are many reasons:

It is bad for the clinician:
- Physicians suffering from burnout are more likely to suffer clinical depression.[5]
- Burnout increases the likelihood to have and act on suicidal ideation.[6]
- Physicians suffering from burnout are more likely to abuse drugs and/ or alcohol.[7]

It is bad for patients:
- Physician burnout can adversely affect patient safety and quality of patient care and contribute to medical errors.[8,9,10,11]
- Physician burnout has been linked with inappropriate prescribing patterns.[12]

It is bad for the medical group:
- Studies show that engaged physicians are 26 percent more productive, generate $460,000 more annual patient revenue, and provide 3 percent more outpatient referrals and 51 percent more inpatient referrals.[13]
- Medical errors and patient lack of satisfaction with medical care provided by burned-out physicians increases the threat of malpractice litigation.[14,15]
- A growing number of physicians are leaving practice prematurely through early retirement and disability.[16] This creates significant financial pressure on the practice, considering replacing a physician can run $500,000 or more when all costs and lost revenue opportunities are considered.[17]

These statistics speak for themselves. Taking steps to engage physicians, and thus decrease physician burnout, will benefit every group of stakeholders.

So What Drives Physician Engagement?

We know from multiple studies and from our work with high-performing physician organizations that there are certain, very specific things that drive physician engagement. Leaders who deliver on these things will have higher engagement among their physicians. They are:

Quality. Physicians need to know that their patients are getting top-notch clinical care, not just while they're at the practice or in the hospital but throughout the entire care continuum.

Efficiency. Physicians want the team members they work with to be prepared with needed information to expedite patient care. This creates more time in the day to spend one on one with patients (which is why they practice medicine in the first place).

Input. Physicians want to be involved in decisions that affect patients and themselves. They want their voice heard—and they want to see follow-through on the input they provide.

Open Communication. Physicians care about transparency and responsiveness. If it impacts patients at all, physicians want to know about it.

Appreciation. Like everyone else, physicians want to hear "thank you" and to be acknowledged when things are going well.

Our advice is simple: Make sure the leaders of your practice can be trusted to do everything possible to meet these five requirements.

Engaging Your Employees

Here's a true story that illustrates what can happen when your employees are not engaged:

One of the organizations we coach is a very large health system that has acquired a number of private practices over the last couple of years. They had 40 percent annualized turnover in clinic staff. Initially, they hired us to work on their patient experience results, but we ended up spending the first year on staff engagement. We literally couldn't do anything else until we helped them fix their turnover problem. They were so busy hiring, training, back-filling, and so forth they had no opportunity to make other improvements.

When we met with them to look at their engagement survey, here's what we found: When the system acquired the independent practices and asked them to comply with their processes, they displaced the practices' clinic managers and put their own people in leadership positions. These new leaders didn't have relationships with the practices' clinicians or staff members.

Even worse, when the health system put these new managers in place, they didn't involve clinicians or staff in the selection process. Not surprisingly, there was no buy-in. They turned the new managers loose to be financial police, meaning they spent most of their time focusing on profit and loss, not on people and relationships.

As turnover accelerated, payroll decreased. This meant that, initially, labor costs were down. From a P&L standpoint, this seemed like a good thing. Yet, as always happens when employee turnover runs rampant, things quickly turned ugly. As soon as leaders trained someone in a skill, that skill holder would walk out the door. As soon as a doctor figured out how to work with a new medical assistant, that medical assistant would leave. This dynamic naturally led physicians to disengage as well.

So for the first year, Studer Group suggested we make employee engagement an important part of all leaders' evaluations by setting goals around it and weighting them at 20-30 percent. We worked with leaders to implement rounding for outcomes and focused on closing the loop on the employee engagement survey results. And we looked for early signs of progress and poured on the reward and recognition. (We'll discuss all these tactics later on in this chapter.)

It worked! Not only did the employee engagement survey results improve, employee turnover plummeted. And as a fringe benefit, physician and patient engagement went up as well, as the employees they interacted with became more engaged.

This organization is not alone. Many medical groups struggle with employee disengagement and it's a big problem. Engaged employees simply provide better, safer patient care. Their engagement goes hand in hand with clinician engagement and is a prerequisite for patient engagement.

Engaging Patients

Ask yourself this question: What's happening when the patient *isn't* in your office or under the direct supervision of another part of your health system? If your words can impact his actions as he goes home to live his life, you know you've succeeded in engaging him.

Matthew's wife, Cindy, is a family nurse practitioner. She tells the following story:

I have a patient who, for years, has struggled with multiple chronic conditions—diabetes, hypertension, hypercholesterolemia, morbid obesity, and asthma. When I first took over her care, she was an uncontrolled type 2 diabetic with an HbA1c north of 11. At our first meeting together, I could see the twin looks of doubt and desperation on her face the minute I opened the door to the exam room. She was quick to tell me that all her previous provider ever wanted to talk about was her diabetes, and gave her a huge "to-do" list—daily insulin injections, multiple oral medications, a new diet and exercise plan, AND a goal of a 100-pound weight loss!

All of this was simply too much for her to face and was overwhelming. It left her unable to make any sort of progress with her diabetes.

I simply sat with her and listened. I was empathetic and validated her frustration. We then identified one single change that she found attainable—decreasing the amount of soda in her diet. Specifically, we agreed that over the next 30 days, she would cut her intake in half—from twelve cans to six. She would replace them with water or unsweetened tea. I would see her again in 30 days and we would see how she progressed.

A month later, when she came back to see me, she was so excited to tell me that she was drinking only four or five cans of soda a day. I congratulated her on her accomplishment and we celebrated. Her spot blood sugar that morning was 250. Although nowhere near goal, it was improved over her usual near 300s.

Her goal for our second month together was to take her Metformin twice daily. She wasn't good about taking her insulin and was rather intimidated by the injections. She thought that taking one tablet twice daily was much more possible. Again, I let her direct our path and my role was mainly to validate and encourage. We planned to meet in 30 days. At our third visit together, she was reporting near perfect compliance with her Metformin, and we saw a further drop in her spot glucose.

And so, we slowly moved forward together, picking small, attainable goals every month, building success upon success. Her A1c slowly came down.

First to 10.3, then to 9.8, and finally to 8. She managed to lose about 20 pounds over the course of a year, kick soda completely, start swimming with her daughter at the local rec center, and mastered using her insulin pen.

She made amazing progress over the course of a year, and I was so proud of her. More importantly, she was proud of herself. She had learned how to break up a nearly impossible goal into small, doable steps by tackling a little at a time. This was so much more satisfying for both of us than it would have been if I just hit her with a laundry list of changes and told her, "Here's what has to happen. Good luck!"

Remember Craig Deao's definition of engagement from the beginning of this chapter? Here it is in action. When a clinician engages a patient, that patient is more likely to do the right thing even when no one is looking.

Unfortunately, the converse is also true. When a healthcare provider fails to engage patients, the consequences can be severe. Keep in mind these sobering statistics from the *New England Journal of Medicine:*
- Forty percent of deaths today are caused by modifiable behavioral issues.
- People with chronic diseases take only 50 percent of prescribed doses... and just 50 percent of patients follow referral advice.
- Fully 75 percent of patients do not keep the follow-up appointments their clinicians schedule with them.[18]

Getting patients engaged really is a "life or death" issue. This is why medical practices must approach engagement as a comprehensive strategy. Remember, engagement starts with leaders and flows down to employees and physicians before it can reach patients. But—again—it's not a one-way street. It also flows back up from patients to physicians and employees and, from there, back up to leaders.

While this book is not meant to be an exhaustive engagement manual, we do want to share a few of the most powerful tools that we've seen jump-start the process for all stakeholders.

Four Foundational Tools That Foster Engagement

There are many practices you can adopt to improve engagement across your organization. We recommend reading Craig Deao's excellent book *The E-Factor* to learn more on this subject. But following are the four tools we have found have had a major *engagement* impact across every medical practice we've worked with.

ENGAGEMENT TOOL #1: Rounding for Outcomes (and Follow-Through). We put this first for a reason: It's the number-one most powerful step you can take to engage your team. Basically, it's a 10-minute conversation held once a month between a supervisor and each of her direct reports. During this one-on-one conversation, the supervisor asks six very specific, very intentional questions:

1. An opening question about them to continue building the relationship. It can be about him specifically, or, even better, a follow-up about a family member from a prior conversation.
2. "What's working well?"
3. "Has anyone done a good job whom I can recognize on your behalf?"
4. "Do you have the tools and equipment you need to do your job?"
5. "Do you have any ideas on systems or processes we could change to make this work better?"
6. And, optionally, a question aimed at helping to hardwire/address a focus across your organization. For example, if you are focused on reducing patient falls (a leading cause of patient injury in medical practice), you might ask: "What are you doing different to reduce patient fall risk, and is there anything I can do to help support you?"

When a leader rounds with employees, she is asking for input. So it's very, very important to follow through on what those employees ask for. If you don't close the loop on this valuable feedback—even if the answer is "I've looked into this and here's why we can't do it at this time"—not only will you *not* engage the employee, you'll damage the relationship. It's worse than if you didn't ask for input at all.

(For more information on rounding for outcomes, visit www.studergroup. com/medical-group/rounding-for-outcomes.)

ENGAGEMENT TOOL #2: Thank-You Notes (and Other Forms of Reward and Recognition). There's a reason your mother insisted you write thank-you notes: It means a lot to a "giver" to receive tangible proof of a recipient's gratitude. Thank-you notes are surprisingly powerful. People save them, cherish them, and get them out when they need an emotional boost. That's why we've always asked senior leaders to hand-write thank-you notes to team members who go "above and beyond" in caring for coworkers or patients.

Imagine receiving a note like this from the CEO:

Your manager Julie told me about all the work you've done in helping our practice reach the 95th percentile on CG CAHPS "Access to Care." Wow! Making sure people can get appointments quickly is vital—not just for the well-being of our practice but for the health and happiness of our patients. Julie asked you to "own" bringing up this CG CAHPS composite, and you did an amazing job. Thanks again. We are fortunate to have you on our team.

Of course, reward and recognition can take many other forms as well. Remember the story of the health system CEO who visited the home of the new ED physician on Christmas Day? That's a great example of reward and recognition. So is giving a small impromptu "bonus" (gift cards to a restaurant or the local movie theater are great) or publicly thanking a physician or employee at a staff meeting. In all its forms, reward and recognition can be a powerful engagement tactic.

(To learn more about thank-you notes, please visit www.studergroup.com/medical-group/thank-you notes.)

ENGAGEMENT TOOL #3: Peer Interviewing. Hiring may be the most important part of establishing tomorrow's culture. Unfortunately, it often gets too little attention. Worse, many of us leaders are not as adept at hiring as we think we are. That's why we recommend that every medical group adopt peer interviewing.

We discussed peer interviewing back in Chapter 3. To briefly review, it's a practice whereby leaders identify high and solid performers to interview their future peers using preset behavioral-based questions. Human resources trains them on how to interview to avoid any legal issues. Then, leaders deploy them to interview only candidates that they (the leaders) have screened and feel are worth consideration.

If the interviewers want to hire a candidate, great: They're automatically invested in making sure their new peer is successful. If they recommend against hiring him, leaders should honor their input and steer clear.

(To learn more about behavioral-based questions and peer interviewing, visit www.studergroup.com/medical-group/peer-interviewing.)

ENGAGEMENT TOOL #4: Engagement Surveys. These surveys are an important part of improving engagement inside your practice. However, they work only if they are handled correctly. Mishandled engagement surveys simply add fuel to the "leadership *says* they care but don't actually listen and change" fire.

Before conducting a survey, it's important to establish the ground rules. Clinical and employee responses should be completely anonymous. What's more, manager results should *not* be factored into performance rating or pay decisions. The idea is for employees to be completely honest and managers to be open to feedback rather than becoming defensive.

Think of engagement surveys as an in-process measure for leaders. The really important measure is the rate of voluntary turnover.

Our role here is not to recommend any particular survey. There are many good surveys in the market, and, in our experience, the survey itself is rarely an area of concern.

Don't Overlook Response Rate

When you get your engagement survey results, don't just look at the engagement rate. Also look carefully at the response rate. We have noticed a disturbing trend in which leaders see the engagement going up and immediately celebrate…not acknowledging or perhaps even noticing that the response rate is plummeting.

One organization we worked with initially shared that 50 percent of their physicians were highly engaged or somewhat engaged. However, when we dug into the data, we found only 40 percent of the physicians had responded to the survey. In other words, 60 percent of the physicians were so *dis*engaged that for one reason or another they did not respond to the survey. When we recalculated engagement—recognizing the non-respondents as disengaged—the engagement rate for the organization was only 20 percent.

Don't be lulled into thinking engagement is improving when response rate is falling!

Here are questions we suggest you ask yourself about your engagement survey follow-through:

- Do leaders acknowledge the results and feedback from the team? Do they say, "Thank you for sharing your feedback so I can improve"?
- Do they involve the team in creating action plans regarding what is going to change?
- Do leaders actually follow through on the action plans?
- Do leaders review progress on the action plans with the teams and do they gain buy-in on next steps?

Here is an example of a change one of our partner practices implemented based on engagement survey feedback:

This practice was communicating organizational changes to everybody at the same time. The problem was the physicians were literally getting told what was happening by the same email that the front desk receptionists received. Because physicians didn't have time to read their email during the day, they were often the last to learn about organizational changes in the medical practice.

Physicians brought this problem to the attention of leaders in the survey. So leadership created a new process to notify physicians about organizational changes the afternoon before the "all hands" communication. As a result of this change, physicians felt in the know. More important, they were in a position to support these changes with their staff.

It's a simple story, isn't it? We agree. However, quite often (more often than you'd believe, in fact), health systems and medical groups will distribute engagement surveys, clinicians and staff will complete them, and then nothing else will happen. As we said regarding rounding for outcomes, follow-through is everything. If you aren't going to respond to feedback, it's better not to ask for feedback in the first place.

Cultures of engagement are not easy to create and sustain. They require diligent hard work and relentless follow-through. Yet making sure all stakeholders are engaged—from leaders to clinicians to employees to patients—is absolutely worth the effort. It's what makes all the strategizing, structuring, training, and refining of processes finally pay off. It's what breathes life into your practice and allows you to bring your mission, vision, and values to full flower as you work to serve your community.

CHAPTER 10

Ensuring the Margin to Live the Mission

"I finally know what distinguishes man from the other beasts: financial worries."
—Jules Renard

How well do you understand the financial management of a medical group? This is an important question. With all the disruptive market changes occurring in healthcare, financial management has become a bedrock competence for any leader tasked with guiding a medical group into an uncertain future.

In the not-too-distant past, medical groups working independently in a largely fee-for-service environment didn't need much financial management. They could see the patient, collect a co-pay, file an insurance claim, put the money in the bank, set up a basic general ledger system, and develop and implement a compensation plan that included a basic expense allocation model. That was about as fancy as they needed to be to operate successfully. Okay, this is an exaggeration but not much of one. Point is, yesterday was a simpler time.

The high-level financial management steps we just listed are still important. However, the degree of financial complexity associated with the practice of medicine has changed dramatically. Never before have medical groups been subject to as much margin pressure driven by payer contract changes, government regulations, and the need to work within larger organizations as they are right now.

As the healthcare industry's transition into value-based payer reimbursement accelerates, it's critical that clinicians and all leaders have a good working understanding of how to manage the business side of a practice. It's these basic mechanics that we've included in this chapter.

The old chestnut of "no margin, no mission" is just as true today as it was yesterday and will be tomorrow. There is a basic formula that medical group leaders must understand:

Revenue – Expense = Margin

In this formula, *revenue* equals all sources of income (typically clinical revenue paid by health insurance and patient co-pays), while *expenses* are the costs that relate to the earning of the revenue (compensation and benefits are typically the largest single costs for a medical group). *Margin* means gross margin and is the difference between the price for the medical group's services and its expenses.

A major working assumption of this chapter is that there is a baseline financial and accounting infrastructure in use by your medical group. This means there are solid general ledger, payroll, and accounts payable systems in place, either through a shared service arrangement provided by a health system, a management services organization, or in stand-alone mode by the medical group.

Going further, it is important that these systems are running on an accrual basis of accounting, that you use a standard chart of accounts (like the MGMA's chart of accounts), and that you have a solid patient accounting and practice management information system in place.

Together, all of these conditions support the management and reporting needs of a sustainable medical group. Most importantly, they make it possible to easily relate revenue and expense at logical levels like physician, specialty, and practice location and provide for other revenue/cost center breakouts that support reporting and analysis rollup capabilities. Without this core infrastructure, the formula provided above will not provide accurate results. One last item: We also assume that there is a formal annual financial audit process in place that includes the medical group.

With those issues out of the way, we can now turn toward what it is that leaders need to know and do to keep on top of the mission/margin issue as it applies to your medical group. The Medical Group Management Association lists the first four of the following areas as key points of focus for the financial performance of a medical group[1]:

- Manage the revenue cycle
- Create and manage an annual budget
- Manage cash flow, accounts payable, and payroll
- Manage the audit process
- Manage health insurance payer contracts*
- Manage physician and provider compensation*

* We added the last two to the MGMA's list as these are important areas of focus and are often unique to medical groups due to their distinct functions and need for specialized staff.

In order to stay on top of these areas of focus, most medical groups, depending on their organization structure, have a chief financial officer position or some similarly titled individual who is responsible for this function along with a staff of specialists who understand finance. Decisions about the number of staff members to include and the specific jobs they do are guided by the size and complexity of the medical group.

Many medical groups have their financial functions divided in some way, with some being held in-house and others handled externally—perhaps via a shared service model with a health system or a management services organization. Often the medical group retains budgeting, revenue cycle management, payer contracting, and physician compensation while the more general accounting, purchasing/payables, and payroll functions are located in a central organization. This works as long as strong transparency, internal controls, and reporting are available to ensure that both sides are performing well.

In a moment we're going to explore each area of focus needed to manage a medical group. But first we want to define three terms: revenue, expense, and margin. (The definitions help clarify why the areas of focus are important.)

Revenue

Revenue to a medical group is largely composed of income generated by clinical care provided and received in payment from patients and/or their insurance plans. However, there are other sources as well. Total revenue is *all* revenue received by the medical group and can include the following:
- Net fee for service revenue
- Capitation payments
- Ancillary revenue (testing)
- Sales of medical supplies
- Biologicals and pharmaceuticals
- Revenue from hospital, nursing home, or home health contracts for medical directorship stipends and other professional service agreements
- Fees for medical-legal expert opinions and testimony
- Other services like aesthetics, prosthetics, hearing aids, glasses, etc. (depending on the practice)

For the purposes of management, revenue expressed as an amount generated by provider is an important metric that we will come back to later in this chapter when we discuss reporting. Here is a quick table generated from the MGMA 2016 Cost and Productivity Survey:

Type	Total Revenue
Primary Care Provider	$1,741,189,421
Nonsurgical Specialist	$1,301,159,571
Surgical Specialist	$1,658,857,302

Expense

Next we define *expense*. Remember, expenses are the costs that relate to the earning of revenue. This is an important concept, especially when a practice thinks through physician and other staff benefit packages and related items. Expenses are typically items such as:

- Compensation and benefits for both physicians and all other staff
- Purchased services
- EHR and IT costs
- Medical, drug, vaccine, and procedure supply costs
- Professional liability and other insurance
- Building and occupancy costs
- Ancillary services costs
- Office supplies

To put this in perspective, take a look at the following bar graph derived from the MGMA 2015 Cost and Revenue Report:

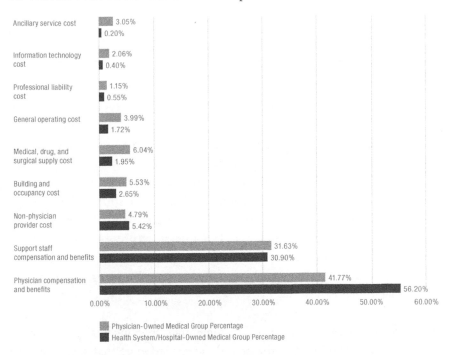

Figure 10.1 | Expense Percentages by Category

It is important to note some things in the data. First (and no surprise), physician compensation and benefits added to other staff compensation and benefits represents the largest items of expense in a medical group. However, it is also important to know that, in general, health system-affiliated medical groups have a different cost profile from that of independent groups. This is because health systems can and do spread costs across a large operation and therefore practice affiliation has a significant impact on the expense profile of a medical group.

Margin

Margin is both the simplest and yet least direct definition in the equation. Although the formula for this critical metric identifies it as the result when you subtract expense from revenue, it is very important to keep in mind the affiliation concept mentioned in the definition of expense. The MGMA has long maintained—and the data generally supports—that independent groups achieve different results from those medical groups affiliated with a health system. Typically, these "different results" translate to lower expenses. It will be important over the course of the value-based-payer-driven transformation of this market to reverse this trend if we're to achieve the goals of reducing cost while improving quality.

Given the high number of physicians who now have some type of employment or affiliation relationship with a health system, operating in that environment creates unique challenges to margins. A simple example is ancillary revenue. Hospital-based medical groups typically have lower revenue generated from ancillary services. Why? Because as part of the integration of the practice, ancillary services like lab, imaging, and infusion service shift to the hospital/outpatient setting. Providing these services at scale—which health systems can do because of their existing ancillary infrastructure—can increase efficiencies and may also support beneficial reimbursement levels. So, it is not unusual for medical groups to report a loss or negative margin due to their larger operational issues.

Therefore, when calculating margin, remember that medical groups affiliated with a hospital bring in direct and indirect revenue that accrues to the overall health system. This is an important concept to keep in mind and will be reviewed later in the chapter. For a key data point on this issue, Merritt Hawkins reports that for 2016, the average physician generated approximately $1.5 million in revenue for the health system that employed her or with which she was affiliated.[2]

Revenue Cycle Management

Managing the revenue cycle in healthcare is a very difficult proposition. Physician revenue cycle management is at least as complex as that associated with other parts of healthcare (hospital, nursing home, home health, etc.). It requires different knowledge from that which it takes to manage a hospital's revenue cycle. On the surface, providing care to a patient, securing information about her means of payment, and receiving payment appears to be very straightforward. However, in reality, this is a complex work process that has a lot of moving parts.

Because the majority of medical care today is provided on a fee-for-service basis where office visits, surgical procedures, and testing are all paid for "per unit," the revenue cycle process is distinguished by a very high number of transactions that have a relatively low level of revenue attached. The keys to success are therefore to standardize and automate work flow and to focus on making systemic changes that reduce rework and wasted effort.

At its most basic level, revenue cycle can be thought of in a "Three Box Model." The first box contains all of the work that goes into accepting a patient appointment, determining how the services are going to be paid for, and then making sure that a charge is generated once the clinical service is provided. This part of the revenue is intertwined with the clinical care process, so it is important that this step is performed well. A major trend that impacts box one and the whole practice is the emergence of high-deductible health plans and efforts by employers and payers to shift a larger share of the cost of care back to patients. Under these models, patients are becoming much more discerning advocates of their care and need a lot more upfront information beyond what they have traditionally received.

The second box is where the handover from the front end of the revenue cycle is made to the back end. In this box resides the true administrative component of the process. This is where the patient's accounts receivable is created, the insurance claim is filed for payment, the statement is sent to the patient, and any co-pays, deductible payments, and ultimately full payment is posted and credited to the medical group for the clinical service. It is one busy part of the process!

The third box is where all the activity around payment, reporting, and process monitoring and management occurs. Here is where medical group leaders need to focus their work. As mentioned, due to the high volume/low revenue nature of physician revenue cycle transactions, the third box is where process monitoring and performance improvement reside. An old saying is in order here: "You can't manage what you don't measure." This is doubly true for the revenue cycle. To ensure that this important business process is performing well, you must have a baseline set of data and key performance metrics that are in place to support communication internally to those involved in the specific workflow between the staff and the physician team.

To illustrate the complexity of the process and to provide more depth to the workings of boxes one and two, here is a high-level summary of the components of a medical group revenue cycle. What should be obvious from this illustration is the number of steps and handovers, the tight linkage with the direct provision of care, and the need to monitor the process continuously to ensure performance. The items listed below and across the processes all need to be understood and closely monitored as part of the "box three" component of the revenue cycle.

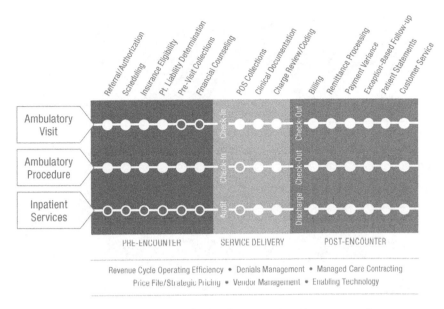

Figure 10.2 | Physician Revenue Cycle: A comprehensive approach
to improving every aspect of the revenue cycle

Here is a high-level picture of the components of the physician revenue cycle that are critical to quality and success in revenue cycle management. In a prior chapter regarding practice efficiency, we highlighted the importance of coding. Here we highlight it again but from a different perspective. Coding is actually just making sure the description of what you did is accurate in the patient's medical record (typically stored in the EHR). For billing purposes, however—because there is a heavy reliance on third party payers like Medicare, Medicaid, and commercial payers—coding needs to be more than just a description of the service. It must be accurate from a payer perspective to ensure timely payment.

The second focus area, ironically, is to make sure there *is* actually a service created from the process of patient care. Even with a strong EHR and practice management system, lost or late charges can still occur given the large volume, fragmented nature, and low revenue yield of each service. Finally, net revenue recovery as represented in the illustration is a more detailed way to explain the importance of the "third box" activities.

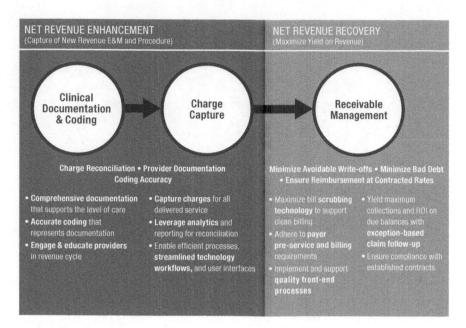

Figure 10.3 | Physician Revenue Cycle: A coordinated end-to-end approach

Budget Management

The preceding section on revenue cycle management took some time as it is a very complex process. Budgets typically are not complex, although there are ways to (unnecessarily) make them that way. As mentioned in the opening of this chapter, revenue minus expense equals margin. The budget is a tool to help you manage what that looks like.

The preferred way to actually build a budget is to start with revenue at the top. In this section you need to look back and project forward by month and quarter what the medical group expects to receive by category. This should include the "large buckets" like clinical revenue but also be broken down by major source—like Blue Cross Blue Shield, PPO, Medicare, etc. Next include your major categories of expense: staff compensation; benefits; fixed and variable costs like rent, medical supplies, equipment, etc.; and then overhead allocations. Overhead usually represents costs for shared services like IT, legal, HR, environmental services, and so forth.

The next step is to sum the revenue and net it against planned expenses to show margin. At this step, physician compensation including planned incentives and benefits should be placed on the budget. From that, the difference between projected revenue and expense should be netted of this physician compensation amount. In this way, you will arrive at what your actual margin is going to be for the practice.

Budget development is often (and rightly) a negotiation process between the major parts of the medical group operation. Therefore it is often an iterative process—and that is a good thing.

During the budget process, medical groups that are acquired or otherwise affiliated with health systems often need some level of mission support to cover the allocated and direct costs of operation. The question of how much this subsidy should be is often a topic of conversation. Benchmarking subsidy levels against MGMA, AMGA, or other sources is important but doesn't tell the full story of what a subsidy should be—or even if there should be a subsidy at all. The absolute number is relevant only to a single group, and benchmarks are helpful only as directional tools.

A more appropriate way to express subsidy is to put direct and allocated expense together with defined "downstream" revenue as one part of the budget development process. This helps leaders gain perspective on what level of subsidy is appropriate. When you tie together downstream revenue, a clear picture emerges regarding whether your physicians really are generating a loss or not. This doesn't mean the medical group is owed the full amount of the downstream revenue; rather, it helps guide the discussion and negotiations that occur during the budget process to lock in a reasonable subsidy number. It is our advice that this also serve as a guide to reduce subsidy over time in order to ensure the financial health of the medical group and the overall health system it is associated with.

This notion of how to think about subsidy is a very important part of the budget process. Overall it will help health systems and medical groups understand what the "real" subsidy is and to develop actionable plans to address any difference between revenue generated and expense consumed.

We find that too many leaders get hung up on the actual number—"I'm investing $300,000 per physician." Well, that might be a bad number. It might be a good number. The point is you can't know without appropriately evaluating and matching all sources of revenue with appropriate uses of expense. This makes for a more transparent budget process even if it is an uncomfortable discussion. Better to understand and acknowledge this issue than to let it fester. It is equally important to share the budget with all physicians who are members of the medical group.

Another key component of the budget management process is cost accounting. This is an emerging area of management (although in reality it is not new). Standard cost accounting has never been a strong area of emphasis for medical groups or for any healthcare organization. However, under a value-based reimbursement model—and in order to compete effectively in the market—it's important that medical groups move to understand their costs. This is not just to control costs and reduce expenses, although that is very important. Rather it is to be able to link cost and quality in a way that meaningfully demonstrates that the service your group provides results in better outcomes at a reasonable price.

As we get deeper into value-driven reimbursement, we really need to know what our costs are within a given budget. As a general rule of thumb, it's believed that 30 percent of all healthcare spending is wasted. This is actually good news for physicians. When they hear that an organization is going to implement cost accounting, they envision a process designed to relentlessly drive down costs without regard to quality or compensation. In a well-run organization this is not the case. The idea is to remove variation and redundancy with the goal of improving quality and preserving margin. If you were to just address the "30 percent waste" factor, you wouldn't have to touch physician salary. The cost accounting process can inform the budget management process and also help other financial and operations management functions.

Cash Flow, Accounts Payable, and Payroll

Managing cash flow, accounts payable, and payroll are primarily day-to-day general accounting functions. While we won't devote a lot of ink to them here, these are important functions. Payroll, for instance, has certain legal and regulatory requirements associated with it, and cash flow is of course very important to ensure proper management of the overall medical group's functions. These areas can be performed internally, via a shared service arrangement, or even outsourced entirely so long as they are maintained with strong controls to ensure the integrity of the medical group's financial position.

Managing the Audit Process

Audits are designed to meet several goals, but in general they are an objective review of operational, clinical, and financial information and accounts to ensure the integrity of the operations and the position of the medical group. The financial audit is done annually and is almost always performed by an independent third party. The goal is to receive a clean audit report, and that is achieved by ensuring that there are strong controls over how funds are managed and used to support the operations of the medical group.

Here are three types of audits that should happen:

1. **Financial.** To ensure the integrity of the financial operations and management of the medical group and is typically performed annually, as described above.
2. **Operational.** To ensure that one or more functions of the medical group are performing with efficiency and effectiveness.
3. **Compliance.** To ensure that various aspects of the medical group, such as revenue cycle, finance, pharmacy, etc., are performing within the requirements of the local, state, or federal regulatory requirements.

All three areas can and should be examined at various times. For example, operational audits can be performed whenever the need arises, while compliance audits should be an ongoing process with formal policies and processes that ensures conformity with the appropriate controlling regulations or laws.

Managing Payer Contracts

Payer contracting has always been a critically important financial management function for medical groups. Management in this context has more than one meaning. The first relates to negotiating with payers for terms and rates and sometimes for patients if the agreement is for capitation or other risk-based contracts. The second is monitoring and management of existing payer relationships to ensure that the payment received is accurate and correct. The negotiation process does require close involvement of knowledgeable and experienced medical group leaders.

For groups that are part of a health system, those designing and negotiating payer contracts too often overlook the uniqueness of individual specialties and primary care services. The medical group management team's role is not to be an adversary to the health system team in this case. Rather, the medical group needs to be an active partner to help achieve better overall contracts that benefit the system as a whole.

As mentioned, it is important that equal time and energy is spent understanding and keeping up with changes in payer rules and regulatory requirements (this is especially true of government programs like Medicare Part B, for instance) as well as other changes that occur on a frequent basis. Someone in your medical group, typically your chief administrative officer, needs to own this responsibility. Simply maintaining this awareness, with guidance and assistance from the revenue cycle team, can ensure that revenue integrity is maintained.

One last aspect of payer contract management is regularly holding a payer mix report and analysis. Monitoring the overall mix of sources of clinical revenue is a great way to keep tabs on the performance of the group as a whole too. Changes in payer mix are important to understand when doing a root cause analysis as they can have a major impact on revenue. (A root cause analysis is simply a way to understand the cause of a problem. It is a Six Sigma concept that can be used to find out what is going on and address the problem "at its root.")

For example, as patients have become more responsible for their care in the form of higher deductibles and co-pays, the character of self-pay as a category in the payer mix has changed and requires new approaches to managing this segment. In this case a root cause analysis could determine the impact of high-deductible and co-pay plans and from that a set of tactics could be employed to make payment easier and more timely for patients with this type of health plan.

Monitoring these changes allows you to maintain the financial health of the medical group and to manage patient engagement, provider satisfaction, and overall service quality.

Managing Physician and Clinician Compensation

Physician and clinician compensation is the single biggest cost that relates to creating revenue for a medical group. We mention both physicians and clinicians because many of the latter group, like nurse practitioners, physician assistants, and others, can and should have performance-oriented compensation plans.

Traditionally, compensation for physicians and some clinicians has been based on how many relative value units are produced in a period of time. In shorthand, this is a production-based compensation model. As a baseline, this can work but it can also be the root of many problems if not implemented in a balanced and thoughtful manner.

Examples of the spectrum of compensation models, as well as their benefits and drawbacks, are illustrated below:

Increasingly Guaranteed Compensation		Increasingly Variable Compensation
Mostly Guaranteed Compensation	**Considerations**	**Mostly Variable Compensation**
Benefits • Compensation spending is easily forecasted and planned for • Plan is easy to understand/implement consistently and fairly • Perceived sense of job security **Drawbacks** • Compensation is not directly tied to performance/productivity • Decreased incentive to align with institutional priorities • May support minimum level work efforts and discourage "entrepreneurship"	An organization's decision on what type of compensation model to implement is dependent on a variety of factors, including: • What model does the organization utilize currently? • What model are direct competitors utilizing in the market? • What benefits are needed to recruit and retain top talent?	**Benefits** • Productivity and performance are easily aligned with institutional proirities • Extra effort is encouraged and rewarded **Drawbacks** • Overhead and fund allocation may be difficult to plan for • May result in competitive environment • Increasingly difficult to implement fairly and consistently

Position on the spectrum of variability should be determined based on the anticipated needs, current priorities, and other circumstances unique to the organization.

Figure 10.4 | Productivity & Compensation Models: Sample Options

Most medical groups have compensation plans that are a) skewed toward variable compensation and b) rapidly moving toward a combination of incentives that are still based on RVUs but that also reward physicians and clinicians who focus on value-based metrics.

What's often overlooked in managing compensation plans, due to the heavy focus on structure, is the administration of the plan. This shortcoming is a little surprising given the magnitude and importance of compensation. The way to overcome this is to develop a small but dedicated team with staffing predicated on the size of the group. This team needs to be equipped with appropriate tools like software and external resources to ensure integrity of the administrative process while also bringing in needed external viewpoints to allow the plan to be appropriately modified and administered. Finally, be sure that there is a regular external legal and audit review of this function in order to ensure compliance with fair market value requirements and related issues.

Reporting and Analysis

Given the nature of medical groups, reporting and analysis is a critically important function. This process must be tied to a solid communication plan. Medical groups are, of course, managed by physicians. The physicians are also the main "unit of production" and therefore need to receive regular and meaningful information about their performance and that of the overall medical group.

The more direct and transparent you can be the better. When people don't understand the issues—or ensure that those on the "other side" understand— they may be perceived as lacking transparency. This can breed resentment. For example, physicians end up saying, "My bonus was X and it should have been Y." This is likely because they don't understand what is driving profit and loss.

There are three kinds of reports every medical group needs.

1. **Operations Reports.** These can occur daily, weekly, or monthly. They tell how many patient visits there have been, how many missed appointments, how many procedures, how many dollars, how many claims. They provide a feel for the pulse and flow of the organizational operations.

2. **Management Reports.** These are monthly reports that tend to be budget-oriented. Essentially, they are variance reports. They say: We *thought we were going to have 100 patients and we had 80. Or we had 120.* The operations committee and key leaders look at both of these reports (operations and management) frequently. Then they reconcile, hold unit meetings of some kind—by location or specialty—and take action to improve performance.

3. **Financial Reports.** These are statements of financial position: income statements, balance sheets, budget pro forma. These tell you: *Here's what we did formally for auditors, bankers, anyone who has interest in our financial position.* These are typically monthly, quarterly, and annual reports. The board looks at these reports each time they meet.

The biggest problem with these reports is that there's no common definition for them. Each report should be classified as to which of the three types it is. What is the frequency with which it's released? Who receives it? What actions are taken in response to the results (such as a variance or a change in volume)?

This goes back to the notion of working to create and maintain a culture of performance improvement. Your reports help support and sustain that effort. At every point in your journey, everyone knows where you stand. Transparency is important as is timeliness of making changes based on the reports.

Determining what to report and what key performance indicators are most important is an endless process. The best approach when determining which metrics to focus on is to use the minimum number possible, report them widely, and make sure they are easy to read and take action on.

Here are some examples of performance metrics that are extremely valuable when the data is good:
- Average expense per patient
  Total expense/monthly or quarterly patient visits
- Average expense per physician
  Same formula as by patient but using total clinical FTE as the denominator
- Average revenue per day
  Adjusted charges for prior quarter/business days in the same quarter
- Average revenue per patient and provider
  Total monthly collections/total monthly patient visits (or CFTE providers)
- Matched net collection rate (generally speaking this should always be 90 or above)
  Gross payments – allowances/gross charges – adjustments
- Overhead analysis (varies by specialty but should not be higher than about 60)
  Total expenses/total revenue

There are other key metrics that need to be quantified and shared about the quality and reputation of a practice. The quality information is an emerging requirement brought about by programs like Medicare with their Quality

Payment Program. Patient engagement and satisfaction measures are another excellent key metric to gather and share with the practice.

There are several keys to good reporting:
- Keep the data accurate by measuring and comparing over time against a baseline and with appropriate comparators
- Format and design simple reports for easy understanding
- Provide wide access to the most important performance information
- Employ a sophisticated and direct communication process about the reports, including what they mean and what progress has been made where improvement is frequently needed

Financial management is a key to quality and a success function of the management team. Focusing on the areas we highlight doesn't guarantee financial success, but if performed with discipline and focus, you can get there. Remember, there is always room for improvement.

There will always be one claim that didn't get filed, a payment that didn't get made or was lost, or some other mistake. You can point a finger in any direction. But so long as there is that needed structure, focus, and appropriate review in the form of reporting and auditing, you will be fine.

Remember too that while financial stability is a critical key to success, it is not the only thing. Don't ever forget that there is a needed balance between mission and margin. Yes, you need margin to keep living your mission—but at no time should the former overshadow the latter. Always, always remember your *why*.

CHAPTER 11

Divergent Medical Groups:
Insights and Leading Practices

"It is not our differences that divide us. It is our inability to
recognize, accept, and celebrate those differences."
Audre Lorde, *Our Dead Behind Us*

We have written this book with a focus on the "typical" medical group of
today and tomorrow. These medical groups tend to employ clinicians from
a multitude of specialties (including primary care) and frequently are either
part of a health system or closely affiliated with one.

However, there are thousands of medical groups that don't fit this definition.
In fact, many groups differ in material ways from these "typical" medical
groups. Even so, many of them tend to organize around certain predictable
alternative organizational models. This chapter addresses several of these
unique medical group types.

Our goal is to ensure we help these divergent medical groups understand
how this book is relevant to them so they can leverage it in their pursuit of
excellence. In addition, many health system leaders may benefit from a better
understanding of some of the different groups with which they are affiliated.

Specifically, we are going to address four unique organizational types that collectively represent over 6,000 medical groups in the U.S. today. These are:

- Federally Qualified Health Centers (FQHCs)/Community Health Centers
- Rural Health Clinics (RHCs)
- Academic Medical Centers (AMCs)
- Clinically Integrated Networks (CINs)

Let's get started.

Federally Qualified Health Centers (FQHCs)/Community Health Centers

What Are Federally Qualified Health Centers?

Federally qualified health centers (FQHCs) are community-based organizations that provide comprehensive primary care and preventive care, including health, oral, and mental health/substance abuse services to persons of all ages, regardless of their ability to pay or health insurance status. They may also be called community/migrant health centers (C/MHCs), community health centers (CHCs), or 330-funded clinics. Non-IHS controlled Indian health clinics may also qualify as FQHCs.

There are over 1,200 community-based FQHC organizations in the United States. By law and policy, their mission is to enhance primary care services in underserved urban and rural communities. In particular, they serve underserved, underinsured, and uninsured Americans, including migrant workers and non-U.S. citizens. And by law they must be either non-profit or public entities.

FQHCs are operated under the supervision of the Health Resources & Services Administration (HRSA), which is part of the U.S. Department of Health & Human Services (HHS). Locally they are directed by a consumer board that must be comprised in majority by patients of their services.

These organizations must provide their services to all persons regardless of ability to pay, and charge for services on a community board-approved sliding-fee scale that is based on patients' family income and size. In return, they receive from the federal government cash grant payments for patients without insurance, cost-based reimbursement for their Medicaid patients, and malpractice coverage under the Federal Tort Claims Act (FTCA).

What Makes Them Unique?

We have been privileged to work with over 50 FQHCs across the U.S. In fact, we have partnered with 7 of the 10 largest as we write this book, and have also worked to create "collaboratives" that bring together multiple smaller FQHCs within a geographic region to share best practices and improve together.

These are perhaps the most mission-driven organizations we have ever been privileged to work with. Their mission, vision, and values are critical to their sustainability. To recruit and retain clinicians and staff, it's critical to never lose sight of this fact. Simply put, people work for FQHCs because it's a calling—rarely can an FQHC afford to compete on salary and benefits with other health providers in its market.

FQHCs are unique among medical practices in being governed by consumer boards that, in the majority, represent their patients. Smart FQHCs turn this to their advantage by recruiting community leaders who bring a diversity of valuable skills to their board, including financial, legal, clinical, and medical practice operational experience. They don't just appoint a board of "yes-sayers" who will blindly approve anything leadership puts in front of them; rather, they find board members who will ask tough questions and help make them a better organization.

FQHCs are also very patient cost-conscious. Perhaps more than in any other care setting, patients and clinicians regularly talk about treatment options with a strong orientation of cost vs. benefit. Recovery time for any treatment is also a serious consideration as many patients do not have jobs that provide "sick time" benefits for recovery.

And perhaps it is therefore not surprising that we have also never met an FQHC CEO who is not incredibly fiscally focused. The mission of serving anyone who needs care, regardless of ability to pay, often strains the organization's financial coffers. That being said, FQHCs need to be careful not to fall into the trap of being penny-wise and pound-foolish.

For example, we recently watched an FQHC cancel their summer picnic because they were behind budget and couldn't afford to close the clinics at 3:00 p.m. on Friday afternoon as planned. When the employees found out the CEO was provided with a leased Lexus to drive as part of his new benefits package the week after the canceled picnic, they were not happy. As a result of this and other similar missteps, the FQHC lost several high performers.

Three Leading Practices of High-Performing FQHCs

We have found that successful FQHCs do certain predictable things. Here, based on our work with these organizations, are three pieces of advice:

Create and Stick to a Comprehensive Strategic Plan. High-performing FQHCs have a three- to five-year strategic plan that guides their senior leadership and board decisions. This does *not* mean they don't occasionally deviate from the plan when a large strategic opportunity comes their way unexpectedly. It does mean they don't chase every shiny penny that rolls across their path. And leaders leverage the strategic plan update process to incorporate outside voices and perspectives, including material input from their board members.

Don't Make Excuses for Results. As Jim Collins taught us in his book *Good to Great*, high-performing FQHCs learn to "confront the brutal facts." They don't let their patient population or FQHC status become an excuse for low-performing results.

We coached one organization where this "woe-is-us" mentality was so bad we had to work with the leaders to stop the blame game and take ownership of results. We implemented a "blame jar" in management meetings. Any leader blaming low-performing results on the patient population, FQHC status, or anything else beyond their control had to put $10 in the jar. Today we are happy to report their leaders hold themselves accountable for the good and poor results—and they now have solid financial results and one of the highest childhood vaccination rates in the country. And as a bonus, the jar helped fund door prizes at that year's employee Christmas party.

Make Clinician and Staff Engagement a Priority. In Chapter 9, we addressed why engagement matters and how you can improve it. And behind every high-performing FQHC that has been able to sustain its results, you will find a highly engaged team. In fact, after working with more than 50 FQHCs, the data is quite clear: Those with high engagement also experience better, more sustainable results in the financial and quality arenas.

Rural Health Clinics (RHCs)

What Are Rural Health Clinics?

The rural health clinic program is designed to support the creation and ongoing delivery of outpatient primary care in underserved rural areas. There are over 4,000 *certified* rural health clinics (RHCs) in the U.S. today.

RHCs are expected to serve rural primary care needs of both Medicare and Medicaid patients. Also they may (and usually do) serve the primary care needs of others in their community. These clinics must be located in areas that are both *rural* (non-urbanized per U.S. Census Bureau) and *underserved* (as determined by the U.S. Health Resources & Services Administration [HRSA]). There is no limitation on how many RHCs may operate in a geographic area. In some rural markets, two or more RHCs may compete with each other.

Unlike FQHCs, these rural health clinics may be public, nonprofit, or for-profit healthcare facilities. They can be owned and operated by either a health system or hospital in their service area (this is the case with most), or they may operate as stand-alone business entities. RHCs that are certified by CMS receive cost-based reimbursement from Medicare and Medicaid that can be higher than standard CMS fee-for-service payments.

RHCs have unique and very specific staffing requirements:
- They may be staffed by physicians, physician assistants (PAs), nurse practitioners (NPs), or certified nurse midwives (CNMs).

- In fact, they must employ at least one NP, CNM, or PA and must be staffed by this professional on-site at least 50 percent of the time they are open.
- RHCs must be "under the medical direction of a physician" who is either an MD or a DO. However, there is no requirement that physicians actually see or treat patients at the RHC.

What Makes Them Unique?

We have been privileged to work with hundreds of health systems and hospitals that operate RHCs. (This includes more than 100 critical access hospitals whose systems include RHCs.) We find working with RHCs to be particularly rewarding for numerous reasons.

First, their unique community mission to provide primary care services to rural and underserved patients brings absolute clarity on "who they serve." This mission connects the clinicians and staff to their purpose—providing primary care to communities that otherwise would not have local care. As we discuss throughout this book, a strong connection to purpose facilitates engagement of all stakeholders, which in turn leads to better clinical outcomes and patient experiences.

RHCs focus on care access challenges for their patients. This often includes the potential benefits of advanced care/diagnostics that require significant travel versus the risks of staying "local." RHCs also often work with patients and families to create unique care plans for potential emergency medical care; pediatric asthma attacks, for example, require a different response when the ambulance takes more than 30 minutes to respond to 911 calls.

Also, RHCs are some of the most team-oriented medical groups we have worked with. This is partly due to the requirement that physicians and advanced practice professionals be included on the clinician team. Also it's partly due to the nature of being in rural and medically underserved areas: Clinicians find ways to team together in the clinic to provide services that in more urban areas would be provided by specialists and other facilities. For example, basic X-rays and 12-lead EKGs are regular components of primary care, as are basic lab tests.

RHCs have unconventional revenue practices. More frequently than in other parts of healthcare delivery, they often negotiate unique financial terms with their patients. For example, a farmer may share some eggs until he can pay the bill when he harvests crops. Or in a Mennonite community, elders may come to the clinic to negotiate and pay their community members' bills.

These clinics often have to carefully think through their revenue cycle with a focus on cash flow. We have worked with more than one RHC that has struggled to address cash flow based on natural market timings in the community—whether it's a rural tourist town where patients earn their money only a few months out of the year, or an agricultural community whose money is tied to harvest season.

Three Leading Practices of High-Performing RHCs

Based on our work with RHCs, we offer the following suggestions for leaders:

Make Sure NPs and PAs Practice at the Full Scope of Their License and Training. As mentioned earlier, leading RHCs may be staffed only by NPs and/or PAs. This allows them to provide high-quality primary care services at lower costs than if they were staffed with physicians. The legal scope of practice for NPs and PAs is important to successfully operating an RHC. In fact, we have learned there is a strong linkage between the scope of independent practice for NPs and/or PAs in a state and the financial health of its RHCs.

Also, provide training to close any needed gaps for the care team. For example, many NPs/PAs can legally provide initial reads of X rays (to be confirmed by radiologists) and appropriate treatment. Yet most NPs and PAs received extremely limited training on reading X-rays in their education.

Be Clear about the Scope of Your Primary Care Practice Services. RHCs often provide "primary care" services that, in urban settings, would be provided by *specialists*. Make sure your community knows this. Be equally clear about which services you don't provide. For example, many RHCs do not provide OB services due to malpractice costs and limited patient demand.

Evaluate services to add to your clinic by carefully considering the financial benefits. Many high-revenue add-on services that make sense in a fee-for-service payment arrangement do not make sense under an RHC's cost-based reimbursement model.

Join Forces with Local Businesses and Institutions to Serve the Unique Needs of Your Community. Financially sustainable RHCs find creative ways to serve both public and private pay patients. For example, we know an RHC that partnered with two local businesses to ensure all their clinicians can provide mandatory commercial driver's license (CDL) physicals. This saves the businesses from sending their employees 45 minutes to a larger town for their regularly required CDL physicals while at the same time providing a solid revenue source for the clinic. The clinic also landed the companies' drug tests and workers' compensation and hiring physicals.

We know another RHC that partnered with their local school to provide an on-site clinic during student registrations to address mandatory vaccinations and sports physicals. This creates a win for all in the rural community. The kids get their mandatory vaccinations and physicals, their parents don't have to schedule time to visit the clinic, the school is able to register the students, and the clinic gets to provide a revenue-generating community service.

Academic Medical Centers (AMCs)

What Are Academic Medical Centers?
The academic medical center (AMC) is a unique entity. AMCs exist to serve several missions. Chief among these is the mission of being a research, education, and training site for individuals learning to become physicians. (Such organizations also train other health professionals like physician assistants, nurses, and so forth. However, these are often referred to as academic health centers, or AHCs. Oregon Health & Science University is one example.)

In order to be truly qualified to teach someone how to be a physician, the professors must be able to actively provide the medical services they teach. So, professors who work at AMCs are MDs or DOs with active licenses to practice medicine. Many AMCs also have strong clinical research programs.

AMC physicians often refer to their personal mission as being like a "three-legged stool," meaning they teach, research, and practice in one or more areas of medicine.

AMCs may have a variety of forms but most possess one or more of the following criteria:

- A medical school affiliation reported to the American Medical Association
- A medical residency program accredited by the Accreditation Council for Graduate Medical Education
- An internship approved by the American Osteopathic Association (AOA)
- A residency approved by the AOA

So, an AMC is an organization that encapsulates a hospital (or hospitals), a school of medicine associated with a public or private university, and, often, a faculty practice plan (FPP) that is affiliated with both the hospital and the school of medicine. The formal definition from the Association of American Medical Colleges (AAMC) of a hospital that is part of an AMC follows:

> *AMC hospital refers to a short-stay, general service, non-federal hospital that has a signed affiliation agreement with a college of medicine accredited by the Liaison Committee on Medical Education (LCME). The hospital must be under some form of common ownership with a college of medicine (or its university) or have the majority of medical school clinical department chairmen serve as the hospital chiefs of service, or have the chairman responsible for appointing the hospital chief of service.*

The AMC structure often includes children's hospitals and veterans' hospitals where there is either ownership or affiliation in place for the clinical professors, residents, or interns (a.k.a. physicians in training) to practice medicine and surgery services as part of the education and sometimes research process.

As part of the AMC, there is often an organization referred to as the faculty practice plan (FPP). At its most basic level, an FPP is a multi-specialty medical group consisting primarily of those faculty physicians and other healthcare professionals who care for patients referred to the AMC. From a financial perspective, they look a lot like any other medical group but do have some unique sources of income, primarily support from the AMC hospital(s), the university for education services, the federal government and industry for research and resident training, and contracts with affiliated organizations like a Veterans Administration hospital.

Organizationally, FPPs follow a couple of different basic models. One is to be an affiliated non-profit entity that follows the IRS rules for this structure, referred to as 501(c)(3) entities (some are 501(a)). In this form, FPPs are typically physician-led organizations with very similar features to any other medical group with the frequent exception that the clinical department chairs are often the leaders rather than other non-chair members. The dean of the school of medicine is often a member in some direct or ex officio manner as well as the CEO or another leader of the AMC hospital. The other option is to simply structure the FPP as a subsidiary entity that is part of the overall school of medicine and is operated as part of the dean's office.

What Makes Them Unique?

If you have followed the description of an AMC, it should be clear that they are very complex organizations that serve multiple missions (teaching, research, clinical service) and have multiple forms and relationships in their medical market. This is true; however, they have several unique features that are very positive. There is an old saying that states that when trying to understand an AMC, don't try and compare it to another AMC because "if you have seen one AMC, you have seen one AMC."

One of the positive features of an AMC is created exactly because of their multi-part mission. Most AMCs offer very high quality access to healthcare for medically underserved patients. Traditionally, AMCs and their affiliated FPPs have made it a point to serve the needs of the poor and to provide care to those patients whose medical condition is unique and requires the expertise of highly trained and capable specialty providers. They also often receive state and federal funds designed to ensure that these types of patients have a place to receive needed care.

Of course, any AMC (like any other health system) can suffer from problems with patient access and care delivery and precisely because of their multiple missions and the complexity of the organization, these problems can be tough to resolve. Regardless, the American health system is reliant on AMCs both to provide new physicians and be active players in their respective healthcare markets either as independent health systems or as part of larger for-profit healthcare providers.

Three Leading Practices of High-Performing AMCs

Fully Integrate with the Community and Your Market. In the past, many AMCs and their faculty practice plans tended to operate "outside" of the geographic and healthcare markets where they were located. This would isolate the AMC and faculty from the real needs of the community. Leading AMCs of today are actively building relationships in their markets and are either acquiring or affiliating with other providers and systems to create more fully functional systems of care. In this way they can provide more cost effective and accessible services for high-end quaternary care on a more seamless continuum with the level of efficiency and timely access we described as being critically important in earlier chapters of this book.

Develop More Efficient and Effective Patient Engagement and Quality Programs. In the past, one old "saw" used to describe AMCs is that they were great places to go for care on the most complex medical problems or trauma needs…but woe be unto those who went there for a common medical problem. The point was that due to their complexity of structure, AMCs could potentially do more harm than good when treating routine problems. Fortunately, this stereotype is dying out.

For the leading AMCs of today, their focus on research and the scientific method has allowed them to make rapid advances in improving patient engagement across the continuum of care. They have also put in place highly effective patient safety and quality programs that—again, because of their mission—they are more than willing to share with others.

In 2016 we worked with a small hospital in the west whose leaders were deciding who to affiliate with in order to continue to provide care in their market. Their choice very quickly came down to an AMC due to its innovative and highly effective patient engagement and retention approaches. These were strategies the AMC developed as part of their overall commitment to quality and effectiveness driven by their tripartite mission.

Help Provide Physicians and APPs to Serve Patient Need. One of the great inefficiencies of the U.S. health system is the imbalance of specialist providers versus primary care providers. Several leading AMCs, especially those affiliated with new schools of medicine and those that are state sponsored, have been taking on this problem. They are focusing their training programs and residency placements on locations like rural areas that need basic primary care provided by a combination of physicians and other advanced practice providers. In this way they are providing needed services that can, over time and with continued focus, help to serve whole neighborhoods and populations to stabilize and improve health.

Clinically Integrated Networks (CINs)

What Are Clinically Integrated Networks?

Clinically integrated networks are "meta-organizations," meaning that they are most often organizations of other organizations. In this case we are talking about logically affiliated medical groups that come together to serve relatively large populations and geographic areas via integrated services and funded by innovative, often risk-based, payer contracts. A CIN may also be composed of hospital members that are part of a (usually) large health system. (Graphics to follow will clarify.)

CINs are not a new phenomenon. However, due to the continuous move of the healthcare market away from episodic, disease-driven, fee-for-service healthcare delivery and toward more consumer-driven and value-based care models, CINs are one of the most active and important developments in the health system and medical group world in some time. Their importance will likely not diminish as we move into the future.

Creating and maintaining a CIN entails the collection and sharing of key data about patients, providers, and their care via sophisticated technology and a common approach to care management. The idea is to coordinate care across the full continuum of sites—acute care, outpatient care, labs, primary care sites, nursing homes, home health, and specialty care, for example—in order to improve the health of a defined population of patients and to be financed by the risk-based contracts mentioned in the first paragraph.

The guiding approach behind the CIN was created by the Institute for Healthcare Improvement and is referred to as the "Triple Aim." Here is an image to illustrate:

Figure 11.1 | The Triple Aim Approach for Clinically Integrated Networks

Here are two formal definitions of what clinical integration means:

> *"The means to facilitate the coordination of patient care across conditions, providers, settings, and time in order to achieve care that is safe, timely, effective, efficient, equitable, and patient-focused."*
> —American Medical Association

> *"An active and ongoing program to evaluate and modify the clinical practice patterns of the physician participants so as to create a high degree of interdependence and collaboration among the physicians to control costs and ensure quality."*
> —Federal Trade Commission

Here is an example of what a clinically integrated network might look like:

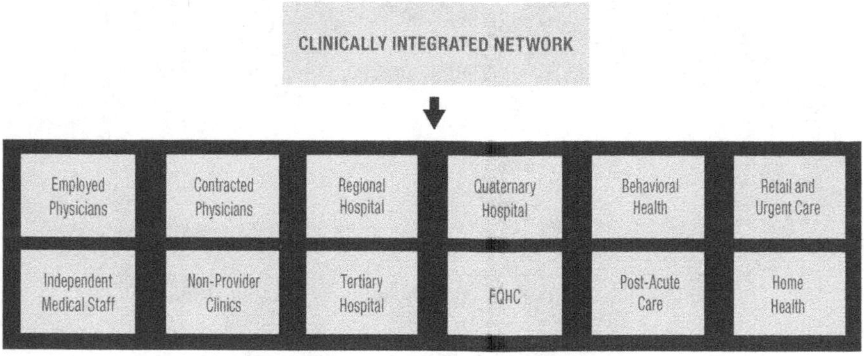

Figure 11.2 | Example of Continuum of Sites That Could Make up a CIN

CINs can be organized in many different ways. However, they are most often structured around a central management services organization (MSO) that provides shared services like IT, billing and collections, payer contracting and management, staffing, finance, etc. The MSO then affiliates with one or more independent practice associations (physician networks) and/or medical groups. The overall organization is managed and led by physicians, especially given the fact that their market objective is to serve defined populations and clinical geographies and improve health while reducing cost. One example of an organization form could be:

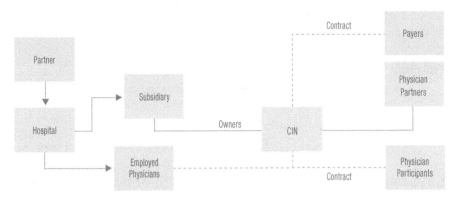

COMMON CHARACTERISTICS
- Physicians can elect board members
- Participation fees will be different for owners than for participants
- All physicians will sign the same membership agreement
- Active participation is required to achieve performance goals
- Profit distribution to owners only, based on company's profits
- Performance rewards will be available to owners and participants based on performance

Figure 11.3 | Sample Organizational Structure: Joint Venture LLC

Here is a summary of the benefits of a clinically integrated network:

Community
- Addresses community needs assessment including behavior health and substance abuse
- Comprehensive view of the population needs to proactively perform outreach

Patients
- Access to high-quality, coordinated, comprehensive care
- Better value for their healthcare dollar
- Greater stability in their relationship with their doctor and hospital
- Effective care management for health and conditions

Medical Groups
- Demonstrate their quality to current and future patients/employers
- Preserve private practice model through mutually beneficial arrangements with hospitals and other providers

- Participate in payment programs that reward quality and efficiency
- Improve performance on physician quality measures

Hospitals
- Develop a more collaborative and efficient relationship with the physician community
- Improve quality and safety outcomes to drive performance
- Opportunity to lower costs while delivering patient-centered care

Employers/ Purchasers
- Ability to more effectively manage the healthcare costs of employees and their dependents through the purchase of more efficient healthcare services
- Lower healthcare costs over the long term throughout the reduction of variation in physician practice patterns

What Makes Them Unique?

Clinically integrated networks are an important and fascinating response to the need to improve healthcare by better organizing resources, managing costs, and improving patient engagement and health outcomes. They allow us to bring together the various major components of the legacy health system— acute care hospitals, medical groups, payers, home health services, LTAC, etc.—in an integrated fashion to treat the needs of patients in a way that is fundamentally different from solutions of the past. Specifically, CINs focus on the patient and his health needs while also keeping a focus on common treatment approaches that can demonstrably improve individual and community measures of health.

Three Leading Practices of High-Performing CINs

Clinically integrated networks are being created to help health systems and their related medical groups transform and thrive in a value-based reimbursement environment to achieve the Triple Aim. There are many leading practices they must have in place, such as care coordination across the patient care continuum; the ability to negotiate, accept, and manage value-based reimbursement contracts that have two-tailed risk; and deep analytic and IT competence to support all of these new practice operations needs.

High-performing CINs:

Recruit and Maintain a Strong Payer Contracting Team. The ability to successfully compete for payer contracts is a core capability of a CIN. To do this, you need a strong team of payer contract management leaders who have deep expertise in physician payer contracts and who also understand risk-based contracting issues and requirements.

We have found that the best CINs take time to find, attract, and retain these individuals and hold them to high standards of performance. They also have strong communication skills. They keep their physician members informed on what the payer market is doing and on how they are working with payers to meet payer requirements. They also work creatively with physicians and payers to develop new products that differentiate the CIN in the market.

Develop Robust IT Capabilities Beyond EHR and Practice Management. In order to be competitive, CIN members need a fully capable IT function. This includes the basics like EHR support, internet services, security, system interoperability, help desk functions, etc. However, it also means being able to bring to bear leading edge analytics and related tools to help members achieve the goals of the Triple Aim. It is not enough to simply share data about patient care. Successful CINs need to be able to analyze data to pin-point opportunities to improve patient health, reduce cost, and track out-comes over time.

Invest in Strong Physician Leadership and Engagement. To be successful, CINs *must* have strong and active physician leaders who partner with and support their physician members. This means more than just developing lead-ing-edge quality measures and related care protocol development. It means ensuring that physicians have strong communication and collaboration skills and the ability to motivate and educate members to achieve a higher level of clinical and business collaboration to live up to the goals of the Triple Aim.

The variations on the medical group theme that we have provided in this chapter are not "all inclusive." Some types of medical groups are single-specialty for-profit organizations such as firms that provide health systems with hospitalists and intensivists. Others are more virtual in nature and are formed to help smaller groups compete. Still we believe reading about these four models of care may be valuable to all types of medical groups.

In general, the medical group sector of the healthcare market is undergoing dramatic and rapid change due to the forces we have outlined in this book. Specifically, we mean the fact that so much care is moving out of the traditional hospital setting, the rise of consumer-driven forces that are changing how medical groups work with their patients, and the ubiquity of technology to provide care in settings unimaginable just five or ten years ago.

The key message is simple: *All* types of medical groups must be able to be readily and easily accessible either via physical location, operating hours, or web portal. They must have strong and flexible infrastructure to support patient-centered care while monitoring quality, expense, and revenue. Above all, they must be able to demonstrate their value to patients and the organizations that pay for care in new and different ways.

Regardless of what category your medical group falls into, we are all focused on the ambulatory market and are facing many of the same market pressures. Thus, we all have the same need for good management, a solid business plan, and great infrastructure in order to function. The time to start moving your organization to compete in this transforming market is now. We hope that by reading about the approach we suggest in this book, you will see a way to take on this challenge and start taking steps in the right direction. We wish you the best results as you move your group forward.

CONCLUSION

Go Forth and Transform

Edison is famously quoted as saying, "I have not failed 700 times. I've succeeded in proving 700 ways how not to build a lightbulb."

A critical point to note is that when Edison set out to invent the lightbulb, he did not start by tinkering with candles. Yet ironically, the solution for his lightbulb turned out to be a carbonized cotton filament—which is a close kin to a candle's wick.

There is an important lesson here. Even as we drive transformation, we must stay connected to the fundamentals. Hopefully, you'll see throughout this book the tapestry of threads that connect today's medical groups to the missions, visions, and values that have inspired healthcare practitioners since the first doctor hung out the first shingle.

Healthcare today is about building the medical group around the patient. It's also about connecting the right patients to the right clinicians in the right care setting and with the right tools and information to deliver high-quality care. It will continue to be about these things tomorrow.

This book is an expression of our sincere desire to provide you with a set of tools that will allow you to avoid 700 failures in transforming your organization into a high-performing medical group. These tools are proven. We believe in them. And we believe leaders who wield them as they boldly stride into the future—not fearlessly (there's no such thing) but despite their fear—will find success at the end of the journey.

That said, don't be *too* invested in avoiding failure. Don't be afraid to lean out over your skis and occasionally take a risk that allows you to fail quickly, cheaply, and safely. When you're creating a better place for clinicians to practice, employees to work, and for patients and families to receive care, you *can't* always play it safe. Leadership is often about shooting for the stars. The people you're working for deserve nothing less.

Vic Arnold
Matthew Bates

ACKNOWLEDGMENTS

First we want to start by thanking our partners and clients. The leaders of these organizations place their trust in us every day to help them with their biggest challenges. We are grateful for this trust and for the wealth of experience we have gained from working with hundreds of medical groups that represent hundreds of thousands of clinicians and millions of patients. Thank you!

We also need to thank our Huron and Studer Group® colleagues who make up our Medical Group team. These dedicated clinicians and administrative team members transform medical groups and their relationships with health systems every day. As the largest and most experienced team in healthcare focused on physicians, they are dedicated to making medical groups better places for clinicians to practice, employees to work, and patients and families to receive care.

Matthew wishes to acknowledge the following, who have inspired and mentored him along his leadership journey:
- Dr. Scott Primack—The first physician leader to ever provide me with a paycheck at Colorado Rehabilitation & Occupational Medicine.
- Dr. Richard Stieg—Who taught me the value of collaboration during our time together at Pinnacol Assurance.
- Dr. Alan Ying—For coaching me in innovation through his work as the founder & CEO of MercuryMD.

- Jean Chenoweth—For teaching me the value of pursuing excellence through her leadership of 100 Top Hospitals® program.
- Doug Schneider—Who mentored me into the world of "servant leadership" at Thomson Reuters.
- BG Porter—Who taught me the value of combining "trust" and "purpose driven work" throughout my tenure at Studer Group.
- Cynthia Bates, FNP—My best friend, wife, and "primary care clinician," who practices at the Three Rivers Medical Clinic.
- Finally, my twins, Zachary & Sophia—Who fuel my passion to leave the world better than I found it.

Vic wishes to acknowledge and thank the following individuals who have both directly and indirectly assisted in his transition into the world of healthcare. This book and its content are the product of input from several people who have helped him understand that patients and physicians are the core to the process:

- Don Tower—My mentor and first boss who spent many years working with faculty practice plans in California, Arizona, Tennessee, and Missouri. His calm demeanor, clear vision, and deep understanding of how to manage and work through the challenges of medical group governance, finance, and hospital/health system relationships were invaluable. I should have paid him rather than the other way around.
- John Heydt, MD, at UC Irvine—He was always a great resource to help me understand how physicians think and best work together.
- Elizabeth Woodcock—For her patience and her guidance with all things medical group and data related.
- David Hunter—Because he is David Hunter. Enough said.
- Last but not least, my wife, Dee Dee Watson—She has managed medical groups for many years—in addition to being a generally calm influence—and is always helpful in sorting out the nuances of day-to-day client situations. Thank you for making a difference in my world.

In addition to the amazing people listed above, the authors want to also expressly thank several colleagues who have been and continue to be invaluable to us and our clients:

- Larry Stuckey—For his collaborations as the leader of our patient access solutions.
- John Tiscornia—For his wisdom, persistence, and knowledge of medical group and health system structures.
- Lynn Grennan, Julie O'Shaughnessy, Todd Hoisington, Mike Collola, Marcel Lisi, Dr. Dan Smith, Kearin Schulte, Dr. Rob Schreiner, Michael Gladson and many other leaders—For their insights and wisdom in guiding our work and making a difference for our partners.

We would also like to thank the Fire Starter Publishing and DeHart & Company teams for your help in capturing and bringing together the best of the best in content between the two of us combined. From managing challenging schedules to mapping out each chapter, you kept us focused and moving ahead. You have worked diligently to ensure that this book will be a valuable resource for physicians and healthcare leaders looking to transform how they practice medicine.

CONTINUE LEARNING

To successfully adapt to a rapidly changing environment, we all need ongoing development in order to improve skill sets and increase knowledge. That's why, in addition to the information you read in *Leading Medical Group Transformation*, we recommend looking at some other leading industry resources to help you better prepare for the transformation of medical groups. Many of the ideas we shared in this book, as well as the knowledge that allows us to do the work we do, are rooted in the following titles:

- *A Culture of High Performance* by Quint Studer. Fire Starter Publishing 2013. ISBN 9781622180035.

- *The E-Factor: How Engaged Patients, Clinicians, Leaders, and Employees Will Transform Healthcare* by Craig Deao, MHA. Fire Starter Publishing 2017. ISBN 9781622180806.

- *Hardwiring Excellence* by Quint Studer. Fire Starter Publishing 2005. ISBN 9780974998602.

- *Healing Physician Burnout* by Quint Studer. Fire Starter Publishing 2015. ISBN 9781622180202.

- *The CG CAHPS Handbook* by Jeff Morris, MD, MBA, FACS, Barbara Hotko, RN, MPA, and Matthew Bates, MPH. Fire Starter Publishing 2015. ISBN 9781622180073.

- *Financial Management for Medical Groups, Third Edition* by Medical Group Management Association. MGMA 2013. ISBN 9781568293950.

- *Performance and Practices of Successful Medical Group Report* by Medical Group Management Association. MGMA 2015. ISBN 9781568296180.

- *Performing an Operational and Strategic Assessment of a Medical Practice, First Edition* by Reed Tinsley, CPA, Joe D. Havens, CPA. John Wiley & Sons 1999. ISBN 9781471299646.

- *Financial and Clinical Benchmarking* by HCIA. Healthcare Financial Management Association 1998. ISBN 9781573720342.

- *The Six Sigma Way Team Fieldbook: An Implementation Guide for Process Improvement Teams* by Peter S. Pande, Robert P. Neuman, Roland R. Cavanaugh. McGraw Hill 2002. ISBN 9780071373142.

- *Mastering Patient Flow: Using LEAN Thinking to Improve Your Practice Operations, Third Edition.* Elizabeth W. Woodcock, MBA, FACMPE, CPC. MGMA 2009. ISBN 9781568292830.

- *Leading Transformational Change: The Physician–Executive Partnership* by Thomas A. Atchison, Joseph S. Bujak. Health Administration Press 2001. ISBN 9781567931617.

- *The Transformation of Academic Health Centers* by Steven A. Wartman, MD, PhD, MACP. Elsevier Academic Press 2015. ISBN 9780128007624.

- *Physician Compensation Plans: State-of-the-Art Strategies* by Bruce A. Johnson, JD, MPA, Deborah Walker Keegan, PhD, FACMPE. MGMA 2006. ISBN 9781568292755.

- "The Strategy That Will Fix Health Care" by Michael E. Porter, Thomas H. Lee. *Harvard Business Review.* October 2013.

- *Competing Against Luck: The Story of Innovation and Customer Choice* by Clayton M. Christensen, Taddy Hall, Karen Dillon, and David S. Duncan. HarperBusiness 2016. ISBN 9780062435613.

- *Dual Transformation: How to Reposition Today's Business While Creating the Future* by Scott D. Anthony, Clark G. Gilbert, and Mark W. Johnson. Harvard Business Review Press 2017. ISBN 9781633692480.

Along with the excellent resources listed above, please visit www.studergroup.com/medical-group to learn more on these subjects and to view the tools mentioned throughout this book.

REFERENCES

Chapter 1:
1. The Physician's Foundation. "2016 Survey of America's Physicians: Practice Patterns and Perspectives." Accessed February 28, 2017. http://www.physiciansfoundation.org/uploads/default/Biennial_Physician_Survey_2016.pdf.
2. Jones Sanborn, Beth. "Digitization, Democratization of Medicine Will Put Patients in Charge of Their Own Healthcare." Healthcare Finance, June 28, 2016. http://www.healthcarefinancenews.com/news/digitization-democratization-medicine-will-put-patients-charge-their-own-healthcare.
3. Porter, Michael E. "What Is Value in Health Care?" *New England Journal of Medicine* 363 no. 26 (2010): 2477-2481. doi: 10.1056/NEJMp1011024.
4. Association of American Medical Colleges. "New Research Confirms Looming Physician Shortage." Association of American Medical Colleges press release, April 5, 2016. https://www.aamc.org/newsroom/newsreleases/458074/2016_workforce_projections_04052016.html. Accessed February 28, 2017.
5. Mullan, Fitzhugh, Edward Salsberg, and Katie Weider. "Why a GME Squeeze is Unlikely." *New England Journal of Medicine* 373 no. 25 (2015): 2397-2399. doi: 10.1056/NEJMp15117076.
6. Association of American Medical Colleges. "New Research Confirms Looming Physician Shortage." Association of American Medical Colleges press release, April 5, 2016. https://www.aamc.org/newsroom/

newsreleases/458074/2016_workforce_projections_04052016.html. Accessed February 28, 2017.

Chapter 3:
1. Collins, Jim. *Good to Great: Why Some Companies Make the Leap...and Others Don't*. New York: Harper Business, 2011.
2. Chen, Walter. "Why Google's Best Leaders Aren't Stanford Grads with Perfect SATs." *Inc.*, July 17, 2014. http://www.inc.com/walter-chen/google-isn-8217-t-looking-for-stanford-and-mit-grads-it-8217-s-looking-for-this-.html.
3. Zismer, Daniel K. and James Brueggemann. "Examining the "Dyad" as a Management Model in Integrated Health Systems." *Physician Executive* 36 no. 1 (2010): 14-9.
4. Barnes, Mary Ann and Donna Lynne. *Kaiser-Permanente's Proposal for a Public-Private Partnership with the Maui Region of Hawaii Health Systems Corporation*. http://www.hhsc.org/wp-content/uploads/Kaiser-Maui-Proposal-Redacted.pdf.

Chapter 5:
1. Institute for Healthcare Improvement. "The Triple Aim Initiative." http://www.ihi.org/Engage/Initiatives/TripleAim/Pages/default.aspx. Accessed March 3, 2017.
2. Johnson, Jean Elizabeth. "An Analysis of Distance Traveled for Healthcare Services Utilizing a GIS." Master's thesis, Saint Mary's University, 1998.

Chapter 6:
1. The Physician's Foundation. "2016 Survey of America's Physicians: Practice Patterns and Perspectives." Accessed February 28, 2017.
2. Wachter, Robert. *The Digital Doctor: Hope, Hype, And Harm at the Dawn of Medicine's Computer Age*. New York: McGraw-Hill Education, 2015.

Chapter 7:
1. National Center for Health Statistics. National Health Interview Study, 2014. Public-Use Date File and Documentation. ftp://ftp.cdc.gov/pub/

Health_Statistics/NCHS/Dataset_Documentation/NHIS/2014/per-sonsx_freq.pdf.

2. National Center for Health Statistics. National Ambulatory Medical Care Survey, 2013. State and National Summary Tables. https://www.cdc.gov/nchs/data/ahcd/namcs_summary/2013_namcs_web_tables.pdf.

3. National Center for Health Statistics. National Hospital Ambulatory Medical Care Survey, 2013. Emergency Department Summary Tables. https://www.cdc.gov/nchs/data/ahcd/nhamcs_emergency/2013_ed_web_tables.pdf.

4. Healthcare Cost and Utilization Project (HCUP). NIS Database Documentation Archive, 2013. www.hcup-us.ahrq.gov/db/nation/nis/nisarchive.jsp.

Chapter 8:

1. Peikes, Deborah N., Robert J. Reid, Timothy J. Day, Derekh, D.F. Cornwell, Stacy B. Dale, Richard J. Baron, Randall S. Brown, and Rachel J. Shapiro. "Staffing Patterns of Primary Care Practices in the Comprehensive Primary Care Initiative." *Annals of Family Medicine* 12 no. 2 (2014): 142-149. doi: 10.1370/afm.1626.

2. Morris, Jeff, Barbara Hotko, and Matthew Bates. *The CG CAHPS Handbook: A Guide to Improve Patient Experience and Clinical Outcomes.* Pensacola: Fire Starter Publishing, 2015. Pg. 7.

3. American Academy of Family Physicians, American Academy of Pediatrics, American College of Physicians, American Osteopathic Association. Joint Principles of the Patient-Centered Medical Home. 2007. http://www.medicalhomeinfo.org/Joint%20Statement.pdf.

4. National Committee for Quality Assurance (NCQA). *Standards and Guidelines for PCSP 2016 Recognition.* Washington: National Committee for Quality Assurance, 2016. PDF e-book.

5. Pryor, Mildred Golden. "Effectiveness and Efficiency." Reference for Business. http://www.referenceforbusiness.com/management/De-Ele/Effectiveness-and-Efficiency.html#ixzz4VPPin5wy. Accessed February 28, 2017.

Chapter 9:
1. Pfeffer, Jeffrey, and Robert I. Sutton. *The Knowing-Doing Gap: How Smart Companies Turn Knowledge into Action.* Boston: Harvard Business School Press, 2000.
2. Grant, Adam M. and David Hoffmann. "It's Not All About Me: Motivating Hand Hygiene Among Health Care Professionals by Focusing on Patients." *Psychological Science* 22 no. 12 (2011): 1494-1499. doi: 10.1177/0956797611419172.
3. Linzer, Mark, Rachel Levine, David Meltzer, Sara Poplau, Carole Warde, and Colin P. West. "10 Bold Steps to Prevent Burnout in General Internal Medicine." *Journal of General Internal Medicine* 29, no. 1 (2014): 18-20. doi:10.1007/s11606-013-2597-8.
4. Shanafelt, Tait D., Omar Hasan, Lotte N. Dyrbye, Christine Sinsky, Daniel Satele, Jeff Sloan, and Colin P. West. "Changes in Burnout and Satisfaction With Work-Life Balance in Physicians and the General US Working Population Between 2011 and 2014." *Mayo Clinic Proceedings* 90 no. 12 (2015): 1600-1613. doi: http://dx.doi.org/10.1016/j.mayocp.2015.08.023.
5. Frank, Erica and Arden D. Dingle. "Self-Reported Depression and Suicide Attempts Among U.S. Women Physicians." *The American Journal of Psychiatry* 156 no. 12 (1999): 1887- 1894. doi: 10.1176/ajp.156.12.1887.
6. Lindeman, Sari, Esa Laara, Heuna Hakko and Jouko Lonnqvist. "A Systematic Review on Gender-Specific Suicide Mortality in Medical Doctors." *The British Journal of Psychiatry* 168 no. 3 (1996): 274- 279. doi: 10.1192/bjp.168.3.274.
7. McCall, Susan V. "Chemically Dependent Health Professionals." *Western Journal of Medicine* 174 no. 1 (2001): 50-4.
8. Shanafelt, Tait D., Katharine A. Bradley, Joyce E. Wipf, and Anthony L. Back. "Burnout and Self-Reported Patient Care in an Internal Medicine Residency Program." *Annals of Internal Medicine* 136 no. 5 (2002): 358- 367. doi: 10.7326/0003-4819-136-5-200203050-00008.
9. West, Colin P., Mashele M. Huschka, Paul J. Novotny, Jeff A. Sloan, Joseph C. Kolars, Thomas M. Habermann, and Tait D. Shanafelt. "Association of Perceived Medical Errors With Resident Distress and Empathy: A Prospective Longitudinal Study." *JAMA* 296 no. 9 (2006): 1071- 1078. doi: 10.1001/jama.296.9.1071.

10. Hall, Louise H., Judith Johnson, Ian Watt, Anastasia Tsipa, and Daryl B. O'Connor. "Healthcare Staff Wellbeing, Burnout, and Patient Safety: A Systematic Review." *PLoS ONE* 11 no. 7 (2016). doi: 10.1371/journal. pone.0159015.

11. Salyers, Michelle P., Mindy E. Flanagan, Ruth Firmin, and Angela L. Rollins. "Clinicians' Perceptions of How Burnout Affects Their Work." *Psychiatric Services* 66 no. 2 (2015): 204-7. doi: 10.11176/appi. ps.201400138.

12. Melville, Arabella. "Job Satisfaction in General Practice Implications for Prescribing." *Social Science & Medicine* 14A no. 6 (1980): 495-499. doi: http://dx.doi.org/10.1016/S0271-7123(80)80055-1.

13. Burger, Jeff and Andrew Giger. "Want to Increase Hospital Revenues? Engage Your Physicians." *Gallup Business Journal* (2014). Accessed July 6, 2016. http://www.gallup.com/businessjournal/170786/increase-hospital-revenues-engage-physicians.aspx.

14. Shanafelt Tait D., Charles M. Balch, Gerald Brchampe, Tom Russell, Lotte Dyrbye, Daniel Satele, Paul Collicott, Paul Novotny, Jeff Sloan, and Julie A. Freishlag, "Burnout and Medical Errors Among American Surgeons." *Annals of Surgery* 251 no. 6 (2010): 995-1000. doi: 10.1097/SLA.0b013e3181bfdab3.

15. Grunfeld, Eva, Timothy J. Whelan, Louise Zitzelsberger, Andrew R. Willan, Barbara Montesanto, and William K. Evans. "Cancer Care Workers in Ontario: Prevalence of Burnout, Job Stress and Job Satisfaction." *CMAJ* 163 no. 2 (2000): 166- 169. http://www.cmaj.ca/content/163/2/166.full.

16. Campbell Jr., Darrell A., Seema S. Sonnad, Frederic E. Eckhauser, Kyle K. Campbell, and Lazar J. Greenfield. "Burnout Among American Surgeons." *Surgery* 130 no. 4 (2001): 696- 705. doi: http://dx.doi.org/10.1067/msy.2001.116676.

17. Smith, Dan. "The Hidden Costs of Declining Physician Engagement." Hardwired Results 14 (2014): 5. https://www.studergroup.com/hardwiredresults14.

18. Parekh, Anand K. "Winning Their Trust." *New England Journal of Medicine* 364, no. 24 (2011): e51. doi: 10.1056/NEJMp1105645.

Chapter 10:
1. Arya, Pawan, James D. Barrett, Owen Dahl, Nancy Enos, David N. Gans, Sarah J. Holt, Sara M. Larch, Daniel D. Mefford, Michael O'Connell, Rhonda W. Sides, Lee Ann Webster, Deborah Walker Keegan, and Robert F. White. *Financial Management for Medical Groups*, 3rd ed. Englewood: Medical Group Management Association, 2014.
2. Merritt Hawkins. 2016 Physician Inpatient/Outpatient Revenue Survey. Coppell: Merritt Hawkins, 2016. February 28, 2017. https://www.merritthawkins.com/uploadedFiles/MerrittHawkins/Surveys/Merritt_Hawkins-2016_RevSurvey.pdf.

ADDITIONAL RESOURCES

About Huron:

Huron is a global professional services firm committed to achieving sustainable results in partnership with our clients. The company brings depth of expertise in strategy, technology, operations, advisory services, and analytics to drive lasting and measurable results in the healthcare, higher education, life sciences, and commercial sectors. Through focus, passion, and collaboration, Huron provides guidance to support organizations as we contend with the change transforming their industries and businesses. Learn more at www.huronconsultinggroup.com.

About Studer Group®, a Huron Solution:

A recipient of the 2010 Malcolm Baldrige National Quality Award, Studer Group is an outcomes-based healthcare performance improvement firm that works with healthcare organizations in the United States, Canada, and beyond, teaching them how to achieve, sustain, and accelerate exceptional clinical, operational, and financial results.

Working together with Huron, we help to get the foundation right so organizations can build a sustainable culture that promotes accountability, fosters innovation, and consistently delivers a great patient experience and the best quality outcomes over time.

To learn more about Studer Group, visit www.studergroup.com or call 850-439-5839.

Medical Group:

Huron and Studer Group have combined our experience from working with hundreds of medical groups over the last decade to form one of the largest and most comprehensive services teams focused on this segment of healthcare. The Medical Group team provides customized approaches to transform medical groups and their partnerships with health systems. Our solutions keep patients at the center, while engaging clinicians and leaders to transform their cultures, develop their leaders, and create sustainable improvements in clinical, operational, and financial results.

Studer Group Coaching:

Studer Group coaches partner with healthcare organizations to create an aligned culture accountable for achieving outcomes together. Working side-by-side, we help to establish, accelerate, and hardwire the necessary changes to create a culture of excellence. This leads to better transparency, higher accountability, and the ability to target and execute specific, objective results that organizations want to achieve.

Studer Group offers coaching based on organizational needs: Evidence-Based Leadership^{SM}, System Partnership, Specialized Emergency Department, Medical Groups, and Rural Healthcare.

Learn more about Studer Group coaching by visiting www.studergroup.com/coaching.

Healthcare Software Accelerators:

Studer Group offers a software suite that aligns directly to the evidence-based framework we work with clients to install. The software accelerators are designed to help organizations get to breakthrough performance faster. In an era of transparency, higher accountability, and visibility, these solutions help healthcare organizations drive consistency. Coupled with Studer Group coaching, this suite of accelerators—Leader Evaluation Manager® (LEM), Provider Feedback System^{SM}, Patient Call Manager^{SM}, and MyRounding®—move the needle for lasting, positive change.

Learn more about healthcare software accelerators by visiting www.studergroup.com/how-we-help/healthcare-software-accelerators.

Educational Conferences:

Studer Group and Huron offer interactive learning events throughout the year that provide a fresh perspective from industry-leading keynote speakers and focused sessions that share evidence-based methods to improve consistency, reduce variance, increase engagement, and create highly profitable organizations. They also provide networking opportunities with colleagues and experts and help participants learn new competencies needed to continuously improve the quality and experience of patient-centered care.

All learning events offer Continuing Education Credits. Find out more about upcoming conferences and register at www.studerconferences.com.

Studer Speaking:

From large association events to exclusive executive training, Studer Group speakers deliver the perfect balance of inspiration and education for every audience. As experienced clinicians and administrators, each speaker has a unique journey to share filled with expertise on a variety of healthcare topics.

This personal touch, along with hard-hitting healthcare improvement tactics, empowers your team to take action.

Learn more about Studer Group speaking by visiting www.studergroup.com/speaking.

Fire Starter Publishing:

Fire Starter Publishing offers intellectual resources for healthcare professionals. We strive to inform healthcare workers of prescriptive to-dos and inspire passion that will encourage action to create change. Our mission is to provide the tools and inspiration to make healthcare better for employees, patients, and physicians.

For over a decade, Fire Starter Publishing has been providing resources to healthcare organizations across the United States, Australia, Canada, China,

New Zealand, and Japan. With more than one million publications in circulation, we are a trusted source for proven tactics and tools to help improve employee engagement, build leadership skills, and improve channels of communication.

Explore Fire Starter Publishing resources by visiting www.firestarterpublishing.com.

ABOUT THE AUTHORS

Victor (Vic) Arnold, MPA

Vic has over 30 years of executive and senior consulting leadership experience in physician organizations in the independent, academic, and large healthcare systems environment. As a managing director with Huron, he has extensive experience in physician practice management and operations efficiency, physician organization alignment, and transformation strategies, along with practice finance and physician compensation.

Prior to joining Huron, Vic owned his own consulting firm that specialized in working with health systems and medical groups as they came together to form larger and more integrated systems. He started in healthcare at the Missouri Medicaid Program managing their provider relations and education program. He went from there to work for academic health systems in their faculty practice plans. This took him to A.T. Still University, Stanford University, and the University of Kansas, where he held executive positions in IT, operations, and overall FPP leadership. He also spent time working as a principal specializing in medical group performance improvement and revenue cycle outsourcing at IDX Systems Corporation and GE Healthcare.

At IDX Systems, he helped develop a revenue cycle outsourcing product for medical groups that was brought to market and transitioned to GE Healthcare.

Vic earned his bachelor of arts from Drury University in political science and economics and has a master's degree in public administration from the University of Missouri-Columbia with mid-career studies that were provided by the Stanford University Graduate School of Business. While at GE, he trained in Six Sigma concepts and approaches to continuous improvement. He has authored numerous articles with regard to medical group practice and is often contacted to provide content to other publications. Vic is married and has a daughter in college at the Kansas City Art Institute.

Matthew Bates, MPH

Matthew Bates is a managing director with Huron where he leads the Medical Group team. The largest and most experienced consulting team focused on physicians in the U.S., they are dedicated to making medical groups a better place for clinicians to work, employees to work, and for patients and families to receive care.

Matthew joined Huron via their acquisition of Studer Group® where he served as the chief product and strategy officer. At Studer Group, he led the application of Evidence-Based Leadership^{SM} to physician organizations, co-developed the Provider Feedback System^{SM} with Quint Studer, and co authored *The CG CAHPS Handbook*. Prior to joining Studer Group, he held leadership roles at Accenture, Thomson Reuters, Solucient, Pinnacol Assurance, and MGMA in the areas of technology, analytics, product marketing, and innovation.

Matthew earned a bachelor of science in healthcare management from the Metropolitan State University of Denver and a master's of public health from the University of Denver. He has also held licensure/certification as a certified nursing assistant (CNA), an emergency medical technician (EMT), a FEMA-certified emergency manager, an OSHA Hazmat first responder, and as a certified professional in healthcare quality (CPHQ).

Matthew resides in Bozeman, Montana, with his wife, Cindy, and their twin children, Zachary and Sophia. They enjoy spending time in the outdoors hiking, camping, biking, and skiing. And when Matthew finds time to slip away, he can be found standing in mountain streams fly fishing for trout.